Coming From Behind

The Mindset of Overcoming Adversity

Gabriel McCurtis, Ed.D., DSL

Coming From Behind: The Mindset of Overcoming Adversity
Copyright © 2022 by Gabriel McCurtis, Ed.D., DSL

All rights reserved. No part of this book may be reproduced or transmitted in any form or by any means without written permission from the author.

ISBN: 978-1-7358359-9-0 (Paperback)
Library of Congress Control Number: 2022914388

Published in the USA by The Vision to Fruition Publishing House

COACHING | PUBLISHING | CONSULTING

www.TheVTFGroup.com

Author Notes

Gabriel E. McCurtis https://orcid.org/0000-0002-8738-745X
I have no conflicts of information to disclose.
Correspondence concerning this article should be addressed to:

Dr. Gabriel E. McCurtis,
P.O. Box 7216, Oxnard, CA 93031, United States

Email: gmccurtis@gmail.com

Abstract

This book is framed around an actual event that happened to Dr. Gabriel McCurtis in the spring of 1975. While a senior at Ventura High School, located in the coastal region of Southern California, Gabriel prepared for the Ventura County Channel League Track and Field Finals that involved several Ventura and Santa Barbara County schools. Gabriel ran the 120-yard high hurdles in 14.8 seconds earlier in the season, which was a good time; however, he experienced a few nasty falls and hit hurdles during the mid-course of the year, which caused him to lose some preseason hurdle races. This book elucidates the various lessons, principles, and changes in Dr. McCurtis' thinking after reaching the second through tenth hurdles that have impacted his outlook on life and have been instrumental in developing his administrative acumen. The book includes insightful strategies and supporting academic theories to provide the reader with an understanding of how to overcome the most difficult circumstances. Dr. McCurtis writes about his experiences in running the hurdle race to demonstrate that winners indeed can come from behind, not only in a track and field event but also in all areas of life that entail hindrances that may lead to failure. The book provides readers with practical strategies for dealing with adversity that can be the difference between being labeled a *hero* or a *zero*.

Table of Contents

Foreword *1*

Introduction *4*

Chapter 1 .... **13**

How to Effectively Deal with Interferences **13**

    Mental Toughness and the Mindset of Championship Competitors 18

    A Meager Upbringing and a Big Opportunity 24

    Reflective Questions 28

Chapter 2 .... **31**

The Response **31**

    Lightning Can Strike Twice 32

    Deliberate Training for Maximal Performance 34

    The Biblical Way for Responding to Challenging Situations 36

    Quit or Finish the Race? The Choice is Yours 37

    What About You? 43

    Reflective Questions 47

Chapter 3 .... **48**

The Pride of Achievement, Not Arrogance **48**

    Who is Watching You from the Grandstands? 49

    Cougar Pride! 50

    The Influence of the Grandstands 52

    The Cameras Are Rolling 54

    Lights, Camera, Action 61

    Reflective Questions 64

Chapter 4 .... **65**

You Can Do It! **65**

    Your View of Yourself and Your Performance 66

    Keep Hope Alive 69

    The Power of Determination 70

    Bull Dog Tenacity and the Mindset of Overcoming Adversity 73

Reflective Questions	78
Chapter 5	***79***
The Awesome Responsibility Involved in Leading Others	***79***
The Need to be a Trustworthy Leader?	80
Are You a Responsible Leader?	84
Your Impact on Others	90
Reflective Questions	94
Chapter 6	***96***
Regaining the Lead	***96***
Regaining the Lead	98
What Will you do After Losing Everything?	100
Keep Your Eyes on the Prize	106
Reflective Questions	110
Chapter 7	***112***
No Time to Rest on Past Laurels	***112***
New Problems Entail New Solutions	115
Now Is Not the Time for Slacking	120
Never Underestimate Your Potential	126
Reflective Questions	130
Chapter 8	***131***
Becoming an Incompatible Force	***131***
Do not Allow Your Competitors to Overtake You	132
Overcoming the Battle of Life	135
Reflective Questions	144
Chapter 9	***146***
Maintaining Your Competitive Edge	***146***
Finish Strong in Your Race	148
Moving Closer to the Finish Line	154
Reflective Questions	156
Chapter 10	***158***
Sprinting Towards the Finish Line	***158***

How are You Doing Now?	161
Clearing the Last Hurdle	164
Sprinting Towards the Finish Line	166
Reflective Questions	171
Conclusion	*173*
References	*176*
Appendix A	*188*
Lessons Learned from Life's Hurdles	*188*
Appendix B	*191*
Trainer's Tips	*191*
Appendix C	*194*
The Mindset of an Overcomer	*194*
Coaching Experience	*197*
About the Author	*199*
About the Publisher	*200*

Foreword

Everyone faces hurdles at various points in their lives. These hurdles manifest in different ways. They exist both internally and externally, they can be unforeseen or glaringly obvious, and they are inevitable. We all have faced struggles and found ourselves disappointed when the *perceptions of where we should be* do not match the *reality of where we are*. The concept behind *Coming from Behind: The Mindset of Overcoming Adversity* is something that can speak to everyone. Most people have felt the pain of losing or falling behind; disappointment, frustration, and self-doubt can easily grip our thinking. However, the greatest fight that any successful person faces is in the battlefield of their minds.

In this book, Dr. McCurtis shares the story of a childhood race—the 120-yard high hurdles—that shaped his mindset, developed his understanding of adversity, and prepared him for his future as an effective leader. Dr. McCurtis places his readers in the middle of the action, seeing the race through his eyes. Every hurdle teaches us a lesson about perseverance and causes us to reflect upon those skills and processes that lead to success. While not all of his readers may identify with the physiological and psychological stress of running an actual race, the narrative is written so that we see through Dr. McCurtis's eyes and are informed by his perspective. Though his story is the foundation and framework for the book.

Dr. McCurtis masterfully interweaves Scripture, research, and practicality such that his readers are inspired and informed. When I read the book, I see the heart of a true man of God who desires to leave a legacy for those who follow. I had the distinct honor of walking with Dr. McCurtis through this journey and personally have witnessed how God has used this small moment in his life to transforming him into the man God called him to be.

It is through this story, and stories like this, that I better understand what the writer of Hebrews meant when he wrote: "Therefore, since we are surrounded by so great a cloud of witnesses, let us also lay aside every weight, and sin which clings so closely, and let us run with endurance the race that is set before us" (*ESV*, Heb. 12:1). Yes, we all experience stumbling blocks and hindrances, but the finish line is attainable, and the prize is worth it. In this race, we *become* whom God has called us to be and influence those whom God has given us to lead.

Coming from Behind: The Mindset of Overcoming Adversity was written to lead readers through a series of hurdles and provide lessons, strategies, and reflective points that help the reader overcome each. Dr. McCurtis reminds us that every race has hurdles, but the prize is worth it all. Thank you, Dr. McCurtis, for that important reminder.

Joshua D. Henson, Ph.D.

Associate Professor of Leadership

Southeastern University

Introduction

The background to this book's writing involved an actual event that happened to me in the spring of 1975. I was a senior at Ventura High School, located in the coastal region of Southern California. I was preparing for the Ventura County Channel League Track and Field Finals, which involved several Ventura and Santa Barbara Counties schools. Earlier in the season, I had run the 120-yard high hurdles in 14.8 seconds, which is a good time. However, I experienced a few nasty falls during the middle of the year when I hit hurdles during the race, causing me to lose.

The Spring rains were very harsh that year, causing a two-week delay in my ability to practice outdoors before the league finals. In addition, during the mid-1970s, all-weather tartan tracks were not as prevalent as they are today in the 21st century. Instead, many Ventura County Channel League schools had asphalt or dirt tracks. Therefore, the conditions that a sprinter or hurdler experienced contributed to slower times than what a decent track athlete could expect while participating in a modern, high-tech athletic field.

The day of the event was like any typical day. I arrived at Hueneme High School, located in Oxnard, California, prepared to compete. Before running in the 120-yard high hurdle race, I performed the usual stretching and conditioning exercises specific to that event. Then, finally, the call came through the loudspeaker that the high hurdle race was next. As I approached the starting blocks, I understood that I was the favored runner to win the event because I entered the race with the season's fastest recorded time and, therefore, was expected to sweep both the high hurdle and low hurdle races.

In the back of my mind, there was the reality that, at the same time in the previous season, I was also favored to sweep both hurdle events; however, I came up short and placed second in both races due to various mechanical errors. At the same time, as I prepared to hear the starter's pistol, I was aware that my girlfriend, now my wife of over 40 years, was in the stands watching the race. I had promised her that I would win both hurdle races and give her my league championship medals. A year earlier, during the Ventura County Channel League Track and Field Finals, I had made a similar promise to win two first-place medals for my girlfriend; however, my second-place finish in both events kept me from fulfilling that promise. Nonetheless, this time, I was confident that she would see me prevail as the Ventura County Channel League Track and Field Champion in my respective events.

Trainer's Tip #1 – There are times when you will not meet your expectations. Do not be alarmed, as this is a part of life.

After settling into the starting block, I heard the starter yell, "On your mark, get set," and then the sound of his starter pistol. As usual, I was the first runner to approach the first hurdle. Unfortunately, as I was in the process of clearing the hurdle, the runner to my right unintentionally spiked my trail leg and interfered in my race.

I was born left-handed, which meant that the leg used when approaching the hurdle was my left leg (i.e., my lead leg), and the next leg to clear the hurdle was my right leg (specifically, my trail leg). In contrast, a right-handed hurdler would lead and trail with their opposite legs. Therefore, when right-handed and left-handed hurdlers run next to one another, contact will occur if both are not highly trained and experienced, leading to one or both hurdlers' interference.

Trainer's Tip #2 - As you journey through life, be prepared to experience unforeseen interferences and occurrences.

Hurdling races move so incredibly quickly because of their ballistic nature. Therefore, you do not have much time to think when something goes wrong. During those occasions, split-second decisions are necessary regarding corrective measures that must happen. One must think or react faster than one can run. In this instance, when I was interfered with by the hurdler running on my right side, my training naturally kicked in, enabling me to continue the race. However, by all rights, I could have stopped running and asked my coach to contest the race on the grounds of interference. All a referee needed to do was to observe that my right knee was bleeding. Had I done so, I may never have written this book.

I figured that the interference I experienced was a one-time deal, so I continued in the race. Unfortunately, the same thing happened again as I went over the second hurdle. I was spiked in the same manner as the first time. Again, I made another split-second decision, realizing that I needed to quickly move away from the interfering hurdler because he would cost me the race. I thought, "I need to get out of here; I need to get out of this mess." I saw that I was no longer in contention for the lead because the rest of the pack had passed by me. At that point, I was just committed to finishing the race. There was no turning back for me now.

As I approached the third hurdle, I caught a glimpse of my girlfriend looking at me as she sat in the bleacher closest to my lane. As I shared earlier, I had promised to give her the two first-place medals I expected to receive as the winner of both hurdle races. Even though it would not have been my fault, I did not want to be embarrassed by losing. So, again, in a split-second dialogue in my head, I said to myself, "Gabriel, you need to get out of this mess." My motivation to win was decisive. I began to rely on *bulldog tenacity*–a deep-seated will and desire to win at all costs. So, I settled down and took a risk, which involved sprinting faster and driving harder towards the fourth hurdle, allowing me to break away and distance myself from the interfering hurdler who hurt my race through multiple interferences.

Looking ahead, I could see that the other runners who moved out in front of me in the race were within a reasonable striking distance. After approaching the fifth hurdle, I had passed some of the slower runners, catching up with the pack's three leaders. By then, I had my stride back and settled back into my race. My determination to win put me on autopilot. I was close to the stands where the audience was sitting, and I could hear the crowd yelling for me and cheering because I was back in contention for winning the race. I also saw camera flashes and a few Ventura High School cheerleaders cheering me on to victory.

By the sixth hurdle, I passed one of the final two hurdlers who was in the lead. My adrenaline was running high as I approached the hurdler who led the race. I maintained the courage needed to challenge him for the lead. I thought, "I know I can win this race!" Three hurdles remained. Having run in many championship races in the past, I realized there was no room for mistakes. I made none. I passed these hurdlers with the speed of a cheetah, a lion's ferociousness, and a gazelle's grace. Once I approached the seventh hurdle, I was in a comfortable lead.

The end of the race was imminent, and I wanted to finish well. Instead of coasting in, my drive and determination made me commit to being a trendsetter. I did not wish to merely win–I wanted to win big. The school record for the 120-yard high hurdles was 14.6 seconds, and I was determined to break that record. After clearing the tenth hurdle, I ended the race in an all-out sprint toward the finish line. After crossing the finish line, I knew I had run a yeoman's race, coming from behind to win, setting a new school record of 14.5 seconds. **The odds I confronted in the race–running on a dirt track not known for speed, experiencing interferences from another competitor twice, and contending with the pain in my right knee from being spiked–taught me that real champions can come from behind.**

In retrospect, I realize what kept me moving forward was an inward compulsion that motivated me to tell myself, "You can do it!" I always strove to train correctly throughout my past training as an athlete. I put in the time to work on my hurdling technique. I sought professional feedback from my coach and other athletes I looked up to regarding my hurdling style. I would train and seek input for corrective adjustments. However, the bulldog tenacity that rose from within made me unwilling to settle for less than my best. I was a McCurtis, the youngest son of my father, Reverend Luther McCurtis.

My dad was known to never give up or throw in the towel. He was infamous for his Bulldog Tenacity–a nickname given to him by a man with whom he did business. He was known to complete projects that looked like they would destroy him. As a pastor, my dad built a church from the ground up in a city known as a graveyard for African American pastors. As a Black man who did not have much money, he purchased an old, dilapidated building and turned it into a multimillion-dollar church campus. The same tenacity resided in me, his third son, Gabriel. **Both tenacity and the favor of the Lord enabled me to come from behind to win the race.** Also, I won the 330-yard low hurdles and came home with two league championship medals for my girlfriend.

The local paper at that time was the *Ventura Star Free Press* which sent a reporter to meet with me and discuss my victory as a double league champion. After meeting with me, the reporter wrote an article saying that, after experiencing some close losses early in the season, I had settled down, matured, and gone on to win the league championship for the hurdles. Therefore, this book will discuss the experiences that enabled me to overcome the barriers I faced while running the 120-yard high hurdles. In addition, I will speak about the seemingly insurmountable obstacles that all people must face during their lives in one form or another. Nonetheless, like me, you, the reader, can also become a champion that prevails and conquers despite life's setbacks. Also, I will give you strategies to build up the winner in you even when you may be coming from behind.

Chapter 1

How to Effectively Deal with Interferences

Hurdle #1: Inadequate Preparation
Avoid entering your competition unprepared so you can compete at your best mentally, physically, and emotionally.

In 1975, during my senior year in high school, I learned that there was more to being an athlete that competed on a championship level than having a solid physique and commensurate athletic skills. I soon understood that an athlete's psychological health and outlook was the support system that undergirded their success or failure. Truly, an athlete's physique and athletic skills represent only a portion of the characteristics needed for success. Hidden below the surface, an athlete's psychological health and outlook can profoundly influence performance.

The first few weeks of the track season were relatively easy, and the races that my high school team competed in were merely preparation for the upcoming league meets. However, as the track season progressed, we began competing with other, more challenging schools. These track meets became increasingly fierce, as did the competition. Our coach taught us not to peak too early in the track season. Though we needed to remain competitive during the early season, it was more important that our skills, speed, and techniques reached their peak during the league finals. Each race was part of a bigger picture.

As we prepared for tough league competition, our coach enrolled us in invitational meets that were much more stringent than our regular season track meets. To qualify to compete at an invitational track meet, an athlete had to meet or exceed a qualifying time. In addition, schools would travel from miles away to bring their top athletes to compete. Because my high school was a CIF Division Four School, we competed with other Division Four high school athletes throughout Southern California. As you would guess, the competition was fierce. **I then learned that while an athlete's athletic training and fitness were significant, the athlete must also maintain a positive psychological outlook to remain competitive.**

Trainer's Tip #3 – To overcome adversity, you must maintain a positive outlook and remain in the game.

During several invitation-only races, I ran against some of the top hurdlers in Southern California. At times, I became so nervous at the beginning of a race that I began hitting hurdles, interfering with my race and results. Consequently, I lost several races in which I should have been more competitive. After those losses, I was devastated because I usually took first place in all my events. It was humbling and educational.

The April rains prevented our team from engaging in any outdoor athletic activities. So instead, our track team workouts, including stretching exercises and cardio conditioning, moved inside the school's gymnasium for two weeks. During the hiatus from competition, I took some time to contemplate some of the factors that caused me to start hitting hurdles. I realized that I had spent more time concentrating on my competitor's race than focusing on my race. I also spent time stretching and soaking my sore muscles in the whirlpool. It was liberating to have time to relax and renew myself as I prepared for the challenges of the upcoming league finals.

Well, the big day arrived. There I was, entering the grounds of Hueneme High School, where the Ventura County Channel League Track and Field Finals convened. As I began my conditioning, I realized that a new Gabriel had entered the field of competition. Who was this new person? The new person maintained a different mindset than his former self, who choked in several hurdling events earlier in the season. This new Gabriel was someone who had determined in his mind that he was a champion.

Some of my track team members informed me that they had overheard some of the other athletes competing in the league finals say that there was a bet out that I would lose both hurdle races. This idle talk did not faze me because I was physically and emotionally prepared to engage in the fiercest competition and emerge victorious. In addition, the two weeks I spent working out in the gymnasium because of the April rains allowed me to develop the mental and emotional fortitude needed for the competition I faced.

A serious athlete realizes the importance of preparation before engaging in any form of competition. Although some athletes are born with a higher degree of natural talent and abilities than others, practice, training, and preparation can give an athlete a competitive edge (Ericsson et al., 1993). Often, an athlete's success or failure derives from the level of confidence attained in preparation for an athletic event (Skinner, 2013). Because most sporting competitions involve physical prowess, a novice would primarily focus on developing their physique (Serrano et al., 2013). However, Morris (2021), the managing director of Believe-Perform, an enterprise founded in 2012 to help others develop positive mental health, contended that after interviewing many professional athletes, coaches, and sports managers about their perceptions of the most important psychological factors necessary for an athlete to excel in sports, they overwhelmingly responded that self-confidence and self-belief were most important.

Mental Toughness and the Mindset of Championship Competitors

Though practice is essential to an athlete's ability to perform, they must equally develop a positive outlook and exercise appropriately for optimal results. For example, Ohuruogu et al. (2016) provided the following observation:

> To attain peak performance in sports competitions, coaches and athletes should not base their prospects on physical training and sports skills alone. Also, the athlete should enter the competition with the proper mindset to achieve optimum performance during sports competitions. (p. 47)

Ikulayo (1990) reported that three psychological factors were necessary for athletes to reach their peak performance during competition: personal, motivational, and mental factors. These three elements work in concert to allow the athlete to rise to a state of physical, mental, and emotional readiness. **Therefore, developing a strategy to enter into competition with the appropriate mindset empowers athletes to compete at their highest level.**

Liew et al. (2019) added to the conversation by identifying other factors involved in the success or failure of an athlete during competition. They contended that an athlete's physical, tactical, technical, and psychological attributes were also essential components in that process. **Moreover, an athlete's psychological state is the most crucial factor in delineating the winners and the losers in competitive endeavors** (Brewer, 2009). Weinberg and Gould (2003) stated that an athlete's mental state of mind during competition against their opponent(s) contributed to over 50% of that athlete's success. Likewise, mental toughness was the most critical factor associated with victory in wrestling (Gould et al., 1987). After questioning 10 Olympic athletes, Gould et al. (2002) identified mental toughness as the single most important psychological characteristic that determined the success or failure of an athlete.

While what constitutes mental toughness is subjective, in its broadest sense, mental toughness references the ability of an athlete to handle the rigors of training and the competitive demands necessary for them to compete effectively and remain resilient (Bull et al., 1996). So, when the call came over the loudspeaker for those athletes competing in the 120-yard high hurdle race to check in with the clerk of the course, I had no idea that my mental toughness, physical prowess, and acquired hurdling skills would be tested by the end of the race.

My preconditioning and warmup went as usual, and I was ready to compete. As the starter had each runner stand behind their starting block in preparation for the start of the race, I was full of anticipation for what lay before me in the upcoming event. After hearing, "on your mark, get set," and then the firing of the starter's pistol, I jetted from the starting blocks like a hungry lion chasing prey. I always believed that the first person over the first hurdle would win the race. Therefore, mentally, I was delighted to approach hurdle number one in the lead.

However, as I descended from the first hurdle, I felt a cold, sharp pain coming from my trail leg, which caused me to stagger between the first and second hurdle. In a split second, I realized that the hurdler to my right had spiked me. The incident shook me for a moment, but I quickly regained my composure. However, on my descent coming off the second hurdle, I felt that familiar cold, sharp pain again as the same hurdler spiked me for the second time. After the second interference, I knew that I could have dropped out of the race and protested the interference with the track umpire, or I could remain in the race and shoot for a comeback because a group of hurdlers had already passed me as I lagged.

I mustered up enough courage to remain in the race because my then-girlfriend of three years, named Deborah Patterson, now my wife of 45 years, was in the stands rooting for me to win. As noted earlier, I promised to bring her back two gold medals, i.e., one medal for the 120-yard high hurdles and another for the 330-yard low hurdles. My conditioning enabled me to remain resilient as I pulled away from the hurdler interfering with my race; the competitive mindset I had acquired during the two-week hiatus from competition enabled me to overcome early interference but ultimately catapulted me to my first-place victory. In addition, the pressure I faced while moving from nearly last place to ending the race as the uncontested Ventura County Channel League Track and Field Champion of the 120-yard high hurdles taught me a life-long lesson, i.e., that real champions can come from behind and still win big.

Howells et al. (2017) reported on a study that focused on an athlete's ability to benefit from difficult situations. After studying Olympic champions, Fletcher and Sarkar (2012) found that optimal sports performance came as the athletes experienced demanding situations. These two authors made the following observation regarding pressure and the performance of Olympic champions:

> Exposure to stressors was an essential feature of ... Olympic champions. Indeed, most participants argued that if they had not experienced certain types of stressors at specific times, including highly demanding adversities ... they would not have won their gold medals. (p. 672)

Hickman et al. (2015) contended that a positive correlation existed between the size of the reward and increased athletic performance–as an athlete sought to achieve the top positions, the larger rewards produced maximum effort (also known as tournament theory). Cowden (2017) reported that while an athlete's performance is essential to their success or failure during competition, just as crucial to the process is the athlete's ability to maintain their performance levels during vital parts of athletic competition. At times during a sports competition, an athlete encounters situations that raise their anxiety level. For example, unexpected adversity during competition may invoke an elevation in anxiety. As athletes maintain similar physical and technical skills during closely contested matches, stress levels maximize. During these occasions, the psychological disposition of an athlete can determine the difference between a successful or unsuccessful outcome. **The athlete's mental toughness is vital in adapting appropriately to the situation and prevailing in the outcome.**

At 18 years of age, competing in a high school track meet, little did I know that many of the principles that have governed my life over the past 46 years would originate from my experience running the 120-yard high hurdles during the 1975 Ventura County Channel League Track and Field Finals. For example, after leaving high school, I was recruited by the University of California Riverside (UCR) to run track on a full athletic scholarship. As you might guess, the competition intensifies at the collegiate level. For example, the height of the high hurdles increased from 39 inches at the high school level to 42 inches at the college level. Additionally, athletes at the collegiate level are often similar in their speed and technique; what often differentiates athletes is their psychological health, outlook, and mental toughness.

A Meager Upbringing and a Big Opportunity

In 1962, my father, an ordained minister, relocated his family from Phoenix, Arizona, to Ventura, California. There, he founded a church on Ventura Avenue on the impoverished side of town. Because he received such a meager income from the newly formed church, dad moved us into a home provided by the Ventura Housing Authority, also known as the Projects. I attended Sheridan Way Elementary School, DeAnza Junior High School, and Ventura High School.

My father and mother encouraged my siblings and me to complete our high school diplomas and secure gainful employment. However, while my mother attended junior college with a desire to become an elementary school teacher, her goal was interrupted as she raised a family of five small children that stair-stepped in age. Therefore, I did not have the necessary influences to prepare me to consider attending a four-year university.

While I took many college-preparatory courses that would enable me to attend a four-year university, I did not have a clear picture in my mind of advancing myself academically. When I was a senior in high school, my mother had begun pressuring me to find a job and advised me that running track would do nothing for my future. However, at the end of my senior year in high school, the head track coach at UCR, Coach Chris, saw me compete during the Southern California CIF Finals in Arcadia, California. He was impressed by my performance and offered me a full athletic scholarship.

It was challenging to leave my humble upbringing on Ventura Avenue to attend one of the top 15 academic institutions in the United States. I struggled to understand the academic jargon used by many of my instructors. At the end of the first quarter of my freshman year, I was on academic probation for the first time in my educational journey. However, I graduated with a Bachelor of Arts Degree in Liberal Studies with a significant concentration in Psychology and a minor in Physical Education.

By the time I graduated with my bachelor's degree in 1980, I was married with two infant children. Not only did I have the pressures of raising my family, pleasing my wife, and working part-time for the Riverside Parks and Recreation Department, but I was also now in the first year of graduate school at UCR, where I sought a California Multiple Subject Teaching Credential to teach elementary school. As I studied with students who had attended higher-ranked high schools and whose parents were well educated and economically stable, I prepared mentally to compete. Though I may have had some factors that placed me at a disadvantage, I challenged myself to meet the obstacles I faced and excel in whatever I put my mind to achieving.

I received my California Multiple Subject Teaching Credential in 1981 and a Master of Arts Degree in Educational Administration in 1983 from UCR. In 2009, I attended a small, private Christian institution named Calvary Chapel University (CCU), where I received a Doctorate of Christian Educational Administration (Ed.D.) and graduated Magna Cum Laude in 2012. My doctoral dissertation was entitled *Administrators' Perceptions of the Effects of Fiscal Reductions on Quality Kindergarten Through Twelfth Grade Instructional Delivery*.

Finally, at the tender age of 60, I attended the California Baptist University located in Riverside, CA, in the Doctor of Business Administration program. However, I underwent back surgery at the end of my first year, which required a few months for me to recuperate. Because I could not continue with my first cohort group, I had to wait a year and resume my educational journey with a new group of students in the second cohort. Once again, being faced with a challenge that would have interrupted my academic pursuit, I researched other notable universities with quality doctoral programs that I could apply to and attend. Hence, I found that the Southeastern University (SEU), located in Lakeland, Florida, had recently begun a Ph.D./DSL program in Organizational Leadership; I applied and was accepted. The writing of this book is the capstone requirement necessary for graduation. At the age of 64, after a second back surgery, I recognized that many achievements in my academic career and in my life, in general, were supported by the inculcation I received during the Ventura County Channel League Track and Field Finals in 1975.

As we proceed to the lessons that I learned after reaching the second through tenth hurdles, I will continue to build upon the strategies and supporting academic theories that enabled me to finish my high hurdle race and win after being faced with many obstacles that would have caused an average athlete to throw in the towel and quit.

However, I learned that winners indeed can come from behind, not only in a track and field event but also in all areas of life that entail hindrances that could result in failure. The strategies you will learn from reading this book and apply to your circumstances could be the difference between being labeled a "hero" or a "zero." As you run your race in life, the choice is up to you.

The Mindset of an Overcomer

Overcomers prevail and conquer their obstacles and hurdles despite setbacks by maintaining a never-give-up and never-give-in mentality.

Reflective Questions

Now that you have become familiar with my story regarding an adverse situation that could have ended in failure yet led to my success as I overcame adversity, it is time for you to review your life's story to determine how you can turn around and change failure into the stepping-stone that can lead to your success. As you ponder over the following questions, please take time to write down your answers with much forethought and reflection:

1. Identify a hurdle (i.e., a situation or an event) that you encountered that led to a setback such as a divorce, job loss, or financial failure that was so devastating that you believed it would cause your life to end in disaster.
2. Did you stop and quit, or did you continue moving forward as you sought to minimize the devastating impact of the hurdle you faced?
3. Do you remember your self-talk? What did you say to yourself?
4. If your response to your hurdle was a response of empowerment, I commend you. However, suppose you have allowed your life's hurdle to cause you to become bitter, frightened, and timid. In that case, I encourage you to reframe your thought processes to include courage in creating a more productive mindset regarding your circumstance(s) and draw upon the champion that lies dormant within to emerge and take charge.

5. In your reflections, begin to see yourself coming out of your stupor with a renewed mindset that your past does not determine your future.

6. Describe what the new you look like and how you would respond to adversity constructively and advantageously.

Chapter 2

The Response

Hurdle #2: Being Unprepared to Handle Contingencies
Expect the unexpected and prepare yourself to overcome all unforeseen problems.

During a recent 10-day stay in the hospital after undergoing a 12-hour lumbar surgery, I recall at least five "code blue" emergency calls coming over the loudspeaker. I was surprised upon hearing the first code blue how quickly the medical staff attending to me ensured I was safe and immediately jetted from my room to respond to the call. Next, I heard other calls such as "code gray" and saw them responded in like manner. After these situations were handled, the nurse would return to my room and inform me of the nature of the emergency. Finally, I learned that code blue meant someone was in medical distress, and code gray entailed a patient becoming violent.

With a background in athletics and as an administrator in the public-school K-12 educational system, I realized that each nurse and accompanying medical provider responded to these emergency calls as part of their mandate as medical professionals, according to their training. Reflecting on my years as a high school and collegiate athlete, I think of the many hours of athletic training spent in preparation for each weekly track or invitational meet across the city and state. That training conditioned both my mind and body to respond on demand as the challenges arose.

Lightning Can Strike Twice

As I shared earlier, another hurdler from an opposing team interfered with me as I cleared the first two of ten hurdles while running the 120-yard high hurdles in the Ventura County Channel League Track and Field Finals in 1975. It was hard enough to adjust and continue in the race after the first interference, but I had no idea I would experience the same mishap over the second hurdle. Early on in my life, I learned that, although it is a very rare occurrence, there are times when lightning strikes twice in the same place. Anyone who witnesses such an occurrence is surprised, if not shocked. However, one should remember that the unexpected and extreme can strike at any time. No one is guaranteed a free ride in life. We cannot control the fact or frequency of being hit with severe circumstances. Problems and challenges will arise without warning, but the real issue in life, as I perceive it, is that when things go wrong, an individual is prepared to deal effectively with the mishap(s).

Trainer's Tip #4 – Your preparedness to adequately face and respond to life's adversities will have an impact on how you deal with them.

A person can respond in many ways when attempting to deal with a problem. Some react in a cowardly manner and run from the situation, while others are brave and face the problem head-on. Naturally, one's level of training to deal with dilemmas will have an impact on how one responds.

During my lifetime, I participated in the Boy Scouts, Naval Sea Cadets, Army ROTC, and organized team sports, to name a few. One thing those organizations had in common was intensive training. During basic training at Fort Knox in Louisville, Kentucky, as I participated in the Army ROTC program, our superiors put my platoon of cadets through rigorous training to prepare us for the battlefield. We engaged in grenade assault training, where I received the marksman's badge, the highest recognition of accomplishment. Moreover, we spent much time at the rifle range shooting targets—where I again received a marksman's badge.

During ROTC training, each cadet received an M16 semi-automatic weapon. We learned to break down and assemble our guns blindfolded through weeks and weeks of training. Every morning, we were subjected to exhaustive physical training. Much of our training entailed running for two to three miles daily and practicing for what was known as the timed obstacle test. As I participated in the training, I learned to proactively mitigate any unforeseen mishaps, which enabled me to continue to complete these events without yielding to the temptation to give up.

Deliberate Training for Maximal Performance

Perhaps you may have wondered why one athlete responds to the sound of a starter's pistol more rapidly than the other participants in a race. One answer is that the runner who responds first may have been born with quicker reflexes. If, however, all the participants in a race are equal in speed and ability, I would contend that the athlete(s) that underwent conditioning and training specifically to react quickly to the sound of a pistol has a competitive edge over the other runners.

Specific techniques for a sprinter to gain maximal ground during the first seven to ten yards of a race are as follows:

1. Remain low and drive hard instead of standing straight up after hearing the starter's pistol.

2. Set the blocks appropriately to provide an explosive start (Bezodis et al., 2019).

3. Vary the progression of their workout from a slow start to a fast finish to lengthen their endurance (Hughes et al., 2017).

Ericsson et al. (2009) reported that a model for deliberate practice that enhanced exceptional performers involved adjusting practice sessions to include extended and intense activities that activated the dormant genes that are asleep within the DNA of all healthy people. The central premise for the model to deliberate practice theory rests on the idea that any performer can attain superior performance through intentional practices and the quality of the training resources used during their training sessions. According to the performer's activity, expert performance levels were attainable after 10,000 hours of structured training over ten years. PGA Golf is one sport where this phenomenon is most visible. I believe that whether a person is an athlete, musician, attorney, or an individual involved in a myriad of other honorable professions, it takes many hours to prepare to be their best if they want to be taken seriously.

The Biblical Way for Responding to Challenging Situations

The *Holy Bible* admonishes the reader to use their trials or hurdles in life to increase their maturity and staying power. For example, James, the brother of Jesus, wrote the following passage:

> Count it all joy, my brothers, when you encounter trials of many kinds because you know that the testing of your faith develops perseverance. Allow perseverance to finish its work, so you may be mature and complete, not lacking anything. (*Berean Study Bible*, 2016, James 1:2-4)

Notice that the reward for overcoming an obstacle is perseverance. Perseverance entails staying power. Had I not effectively dealt with my internal thinking early in the mid-season when

I hit hurdles in some races, my overall performance could have suffered for the remainder of the track season. I could have faltered and failed to win the championship. Rather, I was persistent and remained focused on the upcoming league finals. As I continued training, I developed the mindset that I would finish every race whether or not I experienced interferences. As a result, I learned how to respond proactively to a variety of unanticipated episodes. This enabled me to positively and productively navigate through every challenge and interference.

Trainer's Tip #5 – Perseverance is a crucial factor in overcoming adversity.

Quit or Finish the Race? The Choice is Yours

Many of you who read this book do not have an athletic background and may have no interest in athletics. So, is this book written for athletes? The answer is no. This book is written to provide strategies to people facing difficult obstacles in their lives that will help them to overcome those obstacles. In this book, I reference an episode in my life drawn from an athletic event in which I confronted an obstacle that could have cost me a league championship race. Along with that, I present some coping strategies that allowed me to overcome the challenges that I faced that aided me in reaching my overall goal, which was win that race and give my girlfriend a first-place medal.

The obstacles you now face in life that may have prompted you to read this book may be legal issues, marital problems, mental blockages, or some other circumstance or situation. Whatever the nature of your obstacle(s) and in whatever form they manifest, hurdles are hurdles. But it is vitally important not to stop with that reality. Though the obstacles an individual faces in life are real, it is how the individual perceives the barrier that determines their outcome(s). Roy T. Bennett (2021) wrote the following passage regarding a person having the willpower to reach their dream despite facing obstacles. In his poem entitled "Live the Life of Your Dreams," Bennett wrote, "When you start living your dreams, there will always be obstacles, doubters, mistakes, and setbacks along the way. Nevertheless, there is no limit to what you can achieve" (para.1).

Bennet's poem (2021) elucidates my premise that all life's hurdles are manageable if the person facing them maintains the appropriate mindset and the will to overcome them. I can imagine there are many stories that come to your mind of someone facing insurmountable odds where they faced death or imminent destruction. I can recall stories of people falling off boats and becoming stranded with no food or water for weeks and months at a time, yet they lived to talk about their mishap(s). Moreover, I remember hearing the tales of mothers who somehow gained supernatural strength and ripped off their vehicle's door to save their infant child as they sat trapped in a burning car.

Unfortunately, all people do not get the result that matches their efforts, no matter how herculean. Some people experience the thrill of victory as they overcome great perils in their lives, while many others are not as fortunate and have experienced failure. What, you may ask, is the difference between people who experience success and those who experience failure? Though I strongly believe in divine providence and intervention, I think those individuals who overcome their problems after facing great adversity are those who maintain a victor's mindset. In contrast, the person that does not overcome allows their mindset to be compromised with thoughts of failure.

The foundation of this book has been built on one specific race in which I competed in 1975, but this was not the only situation in which I faced adversity during one of my races that year. Earlier in the track season, during the Ventura Relays, an invitational track meet sponsored by Ventura High School, I learned an invaluable lesson that helped me never to quit a race prematurely but to continue running until I reached the finish line. In the open 100-yard dash, the elite sprinters of Ventura County all competed for a coveted trophy and the prestige of being named the county's fastest male sprinter.

Some of the favorite runners in the race set remarkable times previously during the current track season. As we prepared for the race, it was a toss-up about who would finish first. As we lined up behind our blocks, the starter yelled, "On your mark, get set," and fired his pistol. Like jackrabbits, each sprinter darted out of their blocks. Then, as each of us began running low and driving our feet in the ground for the first ten yards of the race, the starter fired a second shot. We all knew what that meant: someone had jumpstarted in the race, which led to them receiving a strike and facing the possibility of being disqualified and removed from the race if they received a second strike. Slowly, the field of runners returned to their starting blocks. The next three starts ended similarly as three more runners were charged with jumpstarting, causing the starter to stop the race prematurely. Once again, each runner returned to their starting block to await a new start.

One competitor in the race was one of my childhood friends, Austin, who ran for Hueneme High School. After four jump-starts in a row, the entire field of runners grew weary of the false starts. Therefore, many competitors unconsciously expected the next start to end in a false start. Again, the starter lined us up and fired his pistol. For some reason, after sprinting for the first ten yards, just one runner shy of the whole field of runners, including myself, stopped in anticipation of another false start. However, my friend Austin continued to run. We were all caught off guard! When the rest of us finally realized that the start was fair, we turned and jumped back into the race, but we all ran, knowing that Austin would win the first-place trophy. Unfortunately, the only awards that remained were second through fourth place.

What was the secret behind Austin's win? What motivated him to keep running when the rest of the field of runners stopped? After years of training, Austin had been taught not to stop running until he heard the starter's pistol recalling the runners back to the starting line. It is not that the rest of us did not receive the same training; however, Austin made a split-second decision to continue running that resulted in him decisively defeating a field of highly capable sprinters. After being defeated that day by Austin, **I learned never to stop competing in a race due to drawing premature conclusions.**

Now, let us return to the championship race upon which we have been focusing our attention since the inception of this book. After being spiked a second time in the championship race, I was left with only two options: cry foul or remain in the race. I decided to continue in the race and to believe that I still had a chance to win the race and receive the coveted league championship medal—a decision I would learn to appreciate. One of the main factors that caused me not to quit was seeing my girlfriend Deborah sitting in the stands and cheering for me to win. In addition, I knew that my athletic prowess as a hurdler had prepared me to respond to mishaps and interferences appropriately. For example, it was not uncommon for a hurdler to hit a hurdle during a race, which would throw off their stride. Also, a strong gust of wind toppling a hurdle immediately ahead of a runner or having a hurdle placed at the wrong mark was a possibility that could lead to devastating outcomes.

Those weeks and years on the practice field conditioning and developing my form over the hurdles played a significant part in my responding appropriately as I did during that trying circumstance. After the second interference, I pulled ahead of the interfering runner, with my eyes sternly focused on the race ahead, determined to regain the lead. Despite being injured and temporarily discombobulated by the infraction and the resulting pain, I continued to compete.

What About You?

After reading about how I coped with a difficult situation and overcame it, you may wonder are you inspired to consider how you can learn to better manage some of your hindrances? Unfortunately, there is no simple strategy for learning how to adequately cope with painful, debilitating situations that you may confront from time to time; however, you can rejoice because all obstacles have a remedy and an expiration date. You can become highly competent, if not develop an expertise at dealing successfully in the midst of adverse conditions. First and foremost, the most important way of dealing with the problems you may face involves employing a spiritual remedy. Prayer to God in the name of his Son, Jesus Christ, is the appropriate place to start. Jesus was an avid proponent of prayer. To all those who believe in Him, Jesus gave this advice regarding the importance of engaging in prayer in all life's situations and circumstances: "Men ought always to pray and not faint" (*King James Bible*, 1769/2017, Luke 18:1b).

When Jesus said for a believer not to faint, he meant not to give up and quit. While some of the situations you may face in life are hard, you can still experience hope in finding a solution and prevailing in the process. Pastor Chuck Smith (2017), the Calvary Chapel Church organization's founder, stated that there was nothing a person could do before they pray; however, after praying, there are many things a person can do.

Some activities and programs designed to help people respond more appropriately when faced with a complex problem are secular. Though life skills education is a program that begins in grammar school and continues throughout one's young adult years, its principles and application can benefit a seasoned adult. Life skills education aids in an individual's understanding and empowerment, providing an individual the ability to face challenging situations (Slimelane & Mafumbate, 2019).

Prajapati et al. (2016) wrote a paper on life skills education that may be useful to some of you who seek to respond differently to your life's circumstances. Life skills education involves how to improve one's social, emotional, and thinking skills. A list of 10 core life skills is listed as follows:

1. Self-awareness
2. Critical thinking
3. Creative thinking
4. Decision making
5. Problem-solving
6. Effective communication
7. Interpersonal relationships
8. Empathy
9. Coping with stress
10. Coping with emotions (p. 2).

Life skills education equips an individual to handle the pressures of everyday life as they choose to employ positive behavioral strategies. The three broad categories of life skills include thinking skills, social skills, and emotional skills. Social skills include building up one's interpersonal skills, communication, leadership, and advocacy skills. Finally, emotional skills allow a person to become comfortable with who they are and use self-management skills to enhance their coping mechanisms to handle emotions and stress and resist pressures from family and friends.

The Mindset of an Overcomer

Overcomers understand that there are opportunities on the other side of adversity that are not attainable if they quit prematurely and give up in the pursuit.

Reflective Questions

1. What is your self-talk when you confront difficult circumstances?

2. Does your self-talk encourage you to forge ahead or give up?

3. From the list of 10 core life skills germane to life skills education, are there two or three areas for you to learn more about and incorporate into your daily life?

4. How is your prayer life? Do you find time daily to dialogue with the Lord regarding your desire to respond more proactively to negative situations?

5. Now that you have prayed and applied two or three life skill areas strategies into your daily routine, have you noticed any changes in how you view difficult situations? If so, write down some of the new ways that you have learned to respond.

Chapter 3

The Pride of Achievement, Not Arrogance

Hurdle #3: Resisting Arrogant Pride
Arrogance and conceit will try to captivate your soul; resist the temptation at all costs.

Whether in athletics or life, someone is always watching you. In my case, while participating in the Ventura County Channel League Track and Field Championship in 1975, many people were in the grandstands rooting for me to win the 120-yard high hurdle race. The most important person sitting in the stands was my girlfriend, Deborah, and some friends and acquaintances who attended Hueneme High School. In addition, several busloads of cheerleaders and classmates from Ventura High School, where I attended, also were in the stands.

Who is Watching You from the Grandstands?

A reporter from our local newspaper, the *Ventura Star Free Press*, wrote an article about me during the track season. The newspaper article referred to me as the "lone cougar" because my high school mascot was a cougar, and in the more competitive venues, I was the only athlete from my team left to compete. Moreover, once our team entered league and CIF competition, I was the only cougar who placed first in three events: the 120-yard high hurdles, the 330-yard low hurdles, and the 100-yard dash. In my senior year, I was first-team all-league in track and field. It was not uncommon for me to feel pressure to perform at my best from my classmates, friends, and other track and field athletes I competed against.

I remember warming up for a high hurdle race at an invitational track meet when an unknown competitor approached me and said that he had heard that McCurtis would be in the race, and he was scared. Naturally, I responded to him in jest, "I am also scared of running against McCurtis." By the end of the race, I assume he realized that I was the person of his concern. I had built a reputation for myself as a distinguished championship-winning hurdler. As I reflected upon the people sitting in the grandstand watching the track and field events, I recognized that many in attendance knew of my reputation as an elite hurdler and my ability to perform. I did not want to let myself, my girlfriend, or my high school down by performing poorly in any race. It goes without saying, or, as you can imagine, the pressure was on.

Cougar Pride!

As a junior on the Ventura High School varsity football team, we were taught a song by our coaching staff. This song was a song of team pride, also known as "cougar pride." The song goes like this: "I'm a football cougar; I give my all, I fight; IBMA (i.e., I bust my aspirin) and work today for a victory Friday night!" The same cougar pride I learned to exhibit on the football field also profoundly impacted me as an athlete in other sports, such as track and field.

The coaches of Ventura High School instilled cougar pride into every athlete, no matter the sport. **Cougar pride demanded that our behavior and demeanor, whether on-or-off campus,** would inevitably reflect upon our high school, positively or negatively. Hence, we learned to take pride in all we did. The pride that I refer to was not arrogance, in which we looked down on others in conceit. On the contrary, the pride I refer to involved holding high ideals and competing fairly with maximal effort and sportsmanship.

Trainer's Tip #6 – You should always be proud that you did something well (i.e., achievement). However, personal pride should never lead to arrogance or conceit.

As I was interfered with by another runner for the first two hurdles of the race, cougar pride was a factor in spurring me on to overcome that dilemma and stay in the race. As I alluded to in chapters one and two of this book, I was physically equipped to compete at the highest levels of competition and mentally prepared to respond appropriately to all kinds of adversity. Furthermore, the cougar pride instilled in me gave me the extra push to become a winner. It compelled me to foster the strength to continue running despite the interference, persevere through the pain, and become a winner.

Motivated by those factors, I broke away from the interfering runner. I fixed my focus on successfully approaching and sailing uninterrupted over hurdle number three and challenging the pack ahead for the first-place position in the remainder of the race of my life.

Tracey and Robins (2007) researched pride. They found that pride is possibly one of the fundamental emotions found in society as the influence of pride propels a person to attain social status and associated achievements. Authentic and hubristic are the two types of pride found in pursuing social status and related achievements. Authentic pride involves legitimate achievement that produces feelings of accomplishment and success. On the other hand, hubristic pride entails seeking achievement and social status through intimidation and evokes feelings of arrogance and conceit (Cheng et al., 2010).

The Influence of the Grandstands

During the race, the supporters in the stands cheering for me illuminated my understanding of the influence people sitting in the grandstands have on the athlete's athletic performance. In the hurdle race, my lane was so close to the grandstands that I felt like I could reach over and touch the nearest person sitting in the front row. During this event, I could see my girlfriend's face as she watched the race–cheering me on to victory–with a group of friends sitting next to her. I could also hear some of my schoolmates chanting, "Go, Gabe!" I immediately felt that under no circumstances could I let those people down. Therefore, as I approached hurdle three, my mind was filled with the reality that I was not a quitter and that losing the race was not inevitable. It inspired me to conceive the thought that I could win this race. With renewed vigor, my gaze focused steadfastly on hurdle four.

The *Holy Bible* teaches that the believers who die prior to Jesus' second return to earth form a group called "a great cloud of witnesses." They cheer on from Heaven the children of God who remain on the earth to run and finish the Christian race well while they await Christ's return. Hence, the Apostle Paul gave the following warning:

> Therefore we also, since we are surrounded by so great a cloud of witnesses, let us lay aside every weight, and the sin which so easily ensnares us, and let us run with endurance the race that is set before us, looking unto Jesus, the author

and finisher of our faith, who for the joy that was set before Him endured the cross, despising the shame, and has sat down at the right hand on the throne of God. (*New King James Version*, 1982, Hebrews 12:1-2)

The positive affirmations and cheers that emanate from this great cloud of witnesses residing in Heaven are meant to inspire the runners engaged in the Christian race to reach within themselves for higher levels of commitment meant to please our Heavenly Father. We are encouraged not to give up, compromise our lifestyles, and or to quit the race altogether. Likewise, from an earthly perspective, the people in the grandstands offer a source of encouragement to the participants to remain in the race, stay engaged, and finish well.

The Cameras Are Rolling

You will never know who is watching you, so you should always be on your best behavior. For example, while running in the Ventura County Channel League Track and Field Finals, local newspaper reporters, school newspaper reporters, and looky-loos sat in the grandstands. Many of these people had cameras to document the various athletic events. In 1975, cell phones with cameras and videotaping capabilities were not available. Instead, 35-millimeter cameras, reel-to-reel video cameras, and Instamatic cameras were the norm. It was not until a few weeks after I participated in the league finals that I received a package from a local sports reporter containing pictures of me competing in various events.

One picture I still have in my possession captured the moment I regained the lead in the 120-yard high hurdle race. The look of determination on my face still inspires me today as I recognize the tenacity that compelled me to finish the race. In the late 60s and early 70s, there was a television show called *Candid Camera*. The show's objective was to catch a person in a funny or compromised position and snap their picture. After taking the photo, the camera person would yell, "Smile, you're on *Candid Camera*!" Unsuspecting "victims" were captured on film in embarrassing moments while engaged in dumb activities.

Who you think you are and how others view you may not be the same. In psychology, Sigmund Freud argued that each person has an id, ego, and super-ego. These three components of human behavior provide reference points to better understand a person. According to Freud, the id operates at the unconscious level and does not respond to the demands of reality. As the id is self-centered and seeks self-fulfillment, humans create an ego to enable the id's needs to be satisfied through socially acceptable means. Finally, the super-ego strives for perfection as it does not allow the id or ego to get out of hand (Saul, 1940).

From the above analysis of human behavior relating to the id, ego, and super-ego, a person can behave appropriately in the eyes of others while keeping many socially unacceptable desires under control. As in a *Candid Camera* scenario, when a person thinks that they are alone and unmonitored, the real them may come out of hiding, and that person can engage in activities not deemed socially acceptable. However, the dualism in behavior can become problematic when others notice your flaws.

Jesus said that a believer's light is not to be hidden but to shine in a sinful world. He explained that a person does not purchase a lamp to hide its light but for the illumination of their house. Therefore, Jesus admonished all believers to do the following: "Let your light so shine before men, that they may see your good works, and glorify your Father which is in heaven" (*King James Bible*,1769/2017, Matt. 5:13-16).

Do you find it hard to be yourself in front of others? If you answered yes, do you act differently in front of others to find acceptance? I believe that every person has a desire to be accepted by others. Abraham Maslow (1954) reported that each person has a hierarchy of needs. Some of the basic requirements include experiencing safety, security, and acceptance. Maslow asserted that meeting a person's basic needs was a prerequisite for reaching self-actualization.

A person's basic needs include appreciation, need for attention, and acknowledgment from others, to name a few (Maslow, 1954). Singh (2016) explained that human motivation intends to meet individual needs based on five categories from Maslow's model: biological needs, protection, belongingness, esteem, and self-actualization. The physiological, safety, and existence desires were attainable from extrinsic means such as the salary one receives from their employer. In contrast, the need for relationship, understanding, belongingness, attachment, development, self-actualization, and learning needs were met intrinsically by making relational and social contact, independence, accomplishment, and growth opportunities.

In an article entitled *How to be Your Authentic Self: 7 Powerful Strategies to be True,* Soul Salt (2021) presented an approach to prevent individuals from acting pretentiously around others. As I described earlier in this chapter, the images of a group of people sitting in the grandstands filming the real you as you discharge your daily duties are an ever-present reality. **To not be caught off guard in a *Candid Camera* moment, I believe it is essential that what you present to the public is in balance with the real you displayed in private.**

Trainer's Tip #7 – Being authentic requires that your public persona is appropriately aligned to your private self.

As a child, I learned that your reputation is what people say about you, but your character is who you are. Authenticity involves people maintaining a keen awareness of their values and consciousness of who they are at their core. As a result, authentic persons express themselves honestly and consistently to others.

For a person to find their authentic self involves seven strategies (Salt, 2021). The seven strategies are listed as follows:

- Strategy 1: Take a personal inventory of oneself. A person should understand and avoid situations that cause them to act pretentiously. To become an authentic person, you should note the types of people and situations that cause you to experience personal consternation. Moreover, you should note and embrace people and activities that allow you to feel free and alive.

- Strategy 2: Be present in all situations. Doing so is integral to authenticity, as distractions enable people to be unaware of their current state.

- Strategy 3: Build a social support system. Surround yourself with people who are true to themselves and act authentically.

- Strategy 4: Assertively speaking the truth. Being passive or aggressive when communicating does not lead to authentic exchanges.

- Strategy 5: Take authentic daily action. Therefore, daily planning is essential to not become bombarded with other people's priorities.

- Strategy 6: Reflect on your situation.

- Strategy 7: Recognize your internal motivators. For example, in some cases, you must realize when others pressure you to engage in behaviors that involve external forces instead of actions where you are intrinsically motivated.

As I have listened to people who traveled the road to success and reached their goals, I heard some say that their formula for success was that they faked it until they made it. Pretending to be someone you are not entails presenting a false persona that gives others the impression that you are something or someone you are not. **As I stated above, you want others to see the real you; however, when you have flaws, do not try to cover them. Instead, correcting your flaws would help to keep you from acting out of character and pretending to be who you are not.**

When I was in my early 20s, my older brother Michael had a friend who promoted himself as reaching a level of financial success to be envied. This man and his wife were going out of the country for a while and asked my brother if he would care for their car. As they dropped off the automobile, I observed their physical appearance, which was impeccable. The duo, adorned with gold nugget rings, leather coats, and designer jeans accented with a Gucci bag designed for a lady and a leather pouch made for a man, looked like a million-dollar couple.

As young boys coming up, my dad taught my brother and me not to drive other people's cars because we would be responsible if an accident occurred. Unfortunately, my brother Mike did not think it necessary to adhere to my father's advice because, at least on the surface, the husband-and-wife team lived amid a life of luxury and success. After the couple dropped off the car to my brother, he drove it less than a mile, and the transmission fell out. After my brother informed the man and his wife about the status of their car, he soon found himself embroiled in an expensive lawsuit. During the court proceedings, Mike found that his friend and wife had only imitated success and were near financial bankruptcy. This husband-and-wife team evidently lived on the philosophy of we will fake it and let someone break it, then we will sue and lie to get by.

Lights, Camera, Action

I lost vital races earlier in the track season as I hit hurdles that I should have cleared. The April rains forced me to take a hiatus from track and field, settling for stretching, conditioning, and some soul-searching. When I had trouble in the 120-yard high hurdles, I concluded that I was more focused on my competitors' races than on my race. During those moments of introspection, I realized that while I felt like a winner on the inside, I needed that level of confidence to emerge during competition. **At that moment, I understood that to run and win all my future races; I would have to compete in the moment of the heat of the battle with the mindset of a winner, with no interfering distractions.**

Once the league finals came around, I showed up mentally prepared for the performance, and there was no need for me to be pretentious because I knew deep down inside that I was a winner. So, when the "Lights! Camera! Action! moment came as I was competing in the Ventura County Channel League Track and Field Finals; I was physically, mentally, and psychologically prepared to engage in the fiercest competition. As a result, when that sportswriter from the local newspaper snapped my picture as I caught up to and surpassed my competitors after being interfered with early in the race, a look of determination, the effect of bulldog tenacity, and the power of confidence showed on my face during the race. The picture reflected a real overcomer and true champion.

What is your story? Have you encountered barriers in your life that have caused you to believe that there is no hope left for you in your situation? Do you have a determined mind and a willing heart to overcome your adversity? Well, if so, you are reading the right book. I challenge you to take time to engage in some rest, relaxation, and reflection to gain a new perspective. Do not mistake anything I say for meaning that coming back from behind will be easy; it will not be. Nonetheless, it is possible, and it begins with a choice. Maintaining hope or giving up hope are both choices that you control. I did not say that you could do everything alone. Although you have total control of your choices, you cannot do everything on your own. That is why I advocate that you have a close relationship with our Lord and Savior, Jesus Christ, and live a consecrated life that includes daily prayer and Bible study. Through the help of our Lord and the power of the Holy Spirit, there is no mountain, no barrier, no situation, and no hindrance that can stop you from finishing your race like a champion.

The Mindset of an Overcomer

Overcomers are not pridefully self-reliant. They understand that along with their hard work, placing their trust in God for the thing(s) they hope will come to pass is of the utmost importance.

Reflective Questions

1. What are the things associated with your life's barrier(s) that cause you to think about giving up?

2. What are the pros and cons as you ponder your decision to give up or continue?

3. Do you believe God can help you overcome your adverse situations?

4. Can you picture yourself standing at the finish line in victory in the coming months? How does it look and feel?

5. After reviewing the seven steps associated with becoming more authentic, will you take the time to incorporate some of those steps into your life?

Chapter 4

You Can Do It!

Hurdle #4: The Loss of Faith & Hope
Losing your faith and hope results in discouragement that will compel you to give up and quit, but do not give in to its influence.

Is there success on the other side of adversity? The answer is "yes" if the person experiencing an adverse situation changes their thinking from thoughts of dread and gains a different perspective by reframing their mindset to create a beneficial outcome. Broadhurst (1957) and Hebb (1955) researched the relationship between arousal and performance in a person and developed the *inverted-U hypothesis*.

The inverted-U hypothesis view contended that as an individual's arousal state increased, their performance would likewise increase. However, if the arousal state of a person became too excessive, then their performance would decline. While stress would build, if individuals retained confidence in their ability to remain in control, their performance would increase. Conversely, if the stressor exceeded the person's ability to handle it, they would doubt their ability to adequately deal with it, and their performance would deteriorate.

Apter (1982) stated that reversal theory provided answers to the differences seen in successful and unsuccessful athletes as the theory involves their interpretation of the source of their anxiety. According to reversal theory, the source of arousal is interpreted differently according to the person's mental state. For example, viewing pressure from the *telik* state, an athlete is focused on a goal and feels that their state of arousal is related to goal attainment. Conversely, from the *paratelic perspective,* an athlete focuses on their behavior and interprets their state of arousal as excitement. Hardy et al. (1996) argued that individuals could move between one state to another and interpret their arousal differently while in a particular state, thereby influencing their performance.

Your View of Yourself and Your Performance

Over the years, I have learned that no one reason predicts why an individual experiences success or failure regarding their goals. In this book, I have presented many different factors contributing to the varying outcomes a person may experience in obtaining their goal(s). **However, self-efficacy is critical in determining whether individuals will succeed or fail in their quest for accomplishment or victory. Self-efficacy is an individual's conviction of their capacity to succeed in a particular situation. Moreover, their beliefs determine how a person's thoughts, actions, and feelings are derived (Bandura, 1995).**

Trainer's Tip #8 – Your self-talk influences your accomplishments; therefore, keep your self-talk positive.

Cherry (2021) purported that self-efficacy plays a part in how individuals feel about themselves and how successful they are in attaining their goals in life. Bandura (1955) argued that self-efficacy is associated with the self-system that comprises an individual's attitudes, skills, and thinking ability. The self-system's central role involves how one views situations and circumstances and their corresponding response. Thus, self-efficacy is a critical component of the self-system. Finally, self-efficacy influences the goals a person chooses to pursue, their accomplishments, and their performance assessment.

In an article entitled *Self-efficacy and Why Believing in Yourself Matters*, Kendra Cherry (2020), the author, made a list that characterized the differences between people with a strong sense of self-efficacy and those with a weak sense of self-efficacy. She asserted that people with a strong sense of self-efficacy engage in the following behaviors:

- Develop a more profound interest in the activities in which they participate
- Form a stronger sense of commitment to their interests and activities
- Recover quickly from setbacks and disappointments
- View challenging problems as tasks to be mastered (Cherry, 2020).

In contrast, people with a weak sense of self-efficacy reflect the following behaviors:

- Avoid challenging tasks

- Believe that complex tasks and situations are beyond their capabilities
- Focus on personal failings and adverse outcomes
- Quickly lose confidence in personal abilities (Cherry 2020, paras. 11-12).

Keep Hope Alive

Hope has a role in beneficial behavioral modifications that a person makes by supporting goal attainment. The higher a person's hope, the better they perform in education, sports, health, problem-solving, and decision-making. Hope theory is the process of visualizing and establishing goals, creating strategies for goal attainment, and developing beliefs and skills that lead to the motivation necessary to utilize these strategies. Hope and optimism are not synonymous because hope does not generalize about future expectations. Instead, hope involves drawing upon the resources needed to create a positive future state (Magyer-Moe & Lopez, 2015).

After breaking free from the interferences I faced during the first two hurdles of a 10-barrier race, I was physically shaken but not discouraged. Before reaching barrier number three, I had broken free from the distractions. I settled down, sprinted faster, and drove harder towards the fourth hurdle. I passed four of the slower runners in the process, with two faster runners remaining to overtake. My mind was not in distress because I maintained the hope deep within me that I had everything I needed to get back in the lead and win.

I did not panic in this situation because the *Holy Bible* defined faith as "the substance of things hoped for" (*King James Bible*, 1769/2017, Hebrews 11:1a). Thus, hope provides the foundation for faith. I maintained the hope that I could still win the race because the other competitors were within range for me to overtake. Therefore, hope inspired my mind to recalibrate my thoughts, athletic prowess, and mental outlook to get back in the race and win. So, that is just what I did.

The Power of Determination

With renewed faith based on the hope that I could succeed, the power of determination enveloped my body with an infusion of adrenaline. I felt like Captain John Paul Jones when he said, "I have not yet begun to fight!" Captain John Paul Jones was a naval officer who served during the American Revolution. The captain's determination for victory overruled any idea of quitting, and his resolute attitude toward success set the stage for one of the most talked-about naval battles recorded in history (Synder & Morris, 2021).

Chirkov et al. (2003) provided a compelling argument for why I was so motivated and determined to get back in the race and win after the two interferences. These researchers argued that highly motivated athletes engage in sporting activities because of their outcomes, i.e., praise, recognition, and extrinsic rewards. *Extrinsic motivation* is an internalization process based on a continuum of determination that varies from highly self-determined to less self-determined. Extrinsic motivation emanates from an athlete's desire to attain a given outcome, such as winning a prize or avoiding a consequence or punishment.

Yes, I admit that the factors associated with my remaining in the race and not quitting centered on a desire to win because I valued the admiration that would come from my girlfriend, the praise that would come from my classmates, and the distinction of being placed on the all-league first team with an accompanying medal. In addition, winning the race would mean lots of noise coming from the grandstands during the race, with cheers and chants coming from the onlookers. However, because the 120-yard high hurdle race was so fast and ballistic, I could only hear and understand the voice from my internal dialogue. Recovering from the lost time I experienced due to another competitor's interference, self-encouragement was the only form of encouragement I received to get on with the race ahead and win.

The *Holy Bible* provided an account of David and a group of his fighting men returning home from battle to their homes in the city of Ziklag when they found that the Amalekites had invaded their town. The latter burned the city with fire and took as captives all women, children, and possessions (*King James Bible*, 1769/2017, 1Sam. 30:1-31). Once David and his men recognized what the enemy had done, they cried and wept until they had no more tears to weep.

David's men were so upset that they openly spoke about stoning him due to the level of grief that they experienced. However, as David had no one to turn to, he encouraged (i.e., strengthened) himself in the LORD. From my analysis of David, I believe that he could have lost hope and become filled with bewilderment; however, in this instance, he encouraged himself by remembering that there was a higher power in control who could turn around their defeat and make it into a victory. So, once David finished his self-encouragement, he prayed and sought God for a strategy. God told him to fight and pursue the enemy, and he would prevail and recover all that was lost. Thus, David immediately took a group of his men and chased after their enemy until they caught them. After a vicious fight, David and his men won the battle recovering their wives, children, belongings, and the spoils of war they attained from winning the fight.

Bulldog Tenacity and the Mindset of Overcoming Adversity

A bulldog can bite something and lock its jaw. Once that jaw is closed, if the bulldog is mad, it would almost take the intervention of God for that animal to let go of what it is biting. **Therefore, from my perspective, the concept of bulldog tenacity involves a person's ability to grasp hold to an idea, an image, or a goal to be attained, and hold onto it until it becomes a reality. In short,**

bulldog tenacity involves persistence. Yes, I spoke of determination earlier; however, there are times when a person begins their battle with great desire only to fizzle out and release what they had been pursuing. On the other hand, persistence entails a mindset of never giving up whatever the cost.

The mindset promoting resilience is instrumental in overcoming adversity and attaining success. Resilience allows a person to foresee a good outcome despite facing severe threats. A broader look at stability includes any behavior, emotional response, or attribute in response to a social or academic challenge that is positive and beneficial in a person's development, which includes seeking out novel strategies, extending more significant effort, or resolving differences amicably (Yeager & Dweck, 2012). Various factors influence a person's resilience, including environmental factors that contain certain risks and benefits. However, an individual's interpretation of adversity impacts their resilience and is associated with their reaction to a challenge (Olson & Dweck, 2008); the antithesis to stability involves behaviors such as giving up, quitting, cheating, and taking revenge (Masten, 2001).

In most situations I encounter in life, I maintain a never-give-up attitude (i.e., the same attitude I held during my championship race). Yes, at times, quitting may seem like the best option available. However, I have learned over time the meaning of the phrase "winners never quit." Whether needing resilience, bulldog tenacity, or cougar pride, I remained committed to a noble task until its completion.

After ten years of teaching at the elementary level in a K-12 public unified school district, I desired to become a site principal. Therefore, I spent the necessary time fulfilling the requirements needed to be a K-12 administrator in the state of California. Finally, I felt ready to sit at the helm of a public school and provide the necessary instructional leadership conducive to a positive learning environment and educational experience for all students under my charge.

During my last three years in the classroom, I had each student highlight their dream on a T-shirt during Martin Luther King's birthday. The T-shirt read, "I have a dream to become a…". I participated in the activity as well. First, I wrote, "I have a dream to become an elementary school principal." Next, I drew a picture of a red single-room schoolhouse building. Then, on the back of the T-shirt, I wrote the five things I could do to make that dream become a reality.

During the process, I interviewed for several elementary school principalship positions. After one interview, the superintendent of schools called me into his office and critiqued my interview. He told me I needed to demonstrate my instructional leadership skills more effectively. He said that he would help me in my endeavor to obtain my first principalship. First, however, he required that I attend the California Schools Leadership Academy (CSLA) to develop my instructional leadership acumen. My involvement in the Academy included a three-year commitment to demonstrate to the superintendent my level of seriousness in becoming a school administrator.

Facing three additional years of leadership training in the CSLA program required me to prepare my mind to endure a substantial level of delayed gratification. Still, my resilience and desire to move into public school administration outweighed the anticipation /realization of the additional time involved in the temporary delay. I did not see the delay as permanent; instead, I viewed it as an opportunity to better prepare myself for my desired leadership goal. After fulfilling the three-year commitment, I graduated with honors and obtained a principalship immediately after completing the Academy.

These successes that I speak of are not just for me. You, too, are just as worthy of reaching your desired goals. However, one of the things that you must overcome in the process is what I call "stinking thinking." Stinking thinking is the opposite of self-efficacy. Remember, as a prerequisite for reaching your goals, your outlook in life must be bright, and I know you can do it! Reading this book indicates that you are serious about coming from behind and developing a mindset of overcoming adversity. Overcomers maintain an "I still can win attitude" after facing adversity that causes them to fall behind the pack.

The Mindset of an Overcomer

Overcomers maintain an "I still can win" attitude after facing adversity that caused them to fall behind the pack.

Reflective Questions

1. Do you see success or failure on the other side of adversity? Why? Write down your thoughts as to why you chose your answer.

2. Do you have a strong or weak sense of self-efficacy? Review the characteristics of an individual with a strong or weak sense of self-efficacy. If you conclude that you have weak self-efficacy, what do you need to do to move from your current position to the other category? Develop a plan and stick with it.

3. Do you believe that God can help you to overcome adverse situations? Why or why not?

4. Can you picture yourself standing at the finish line in victory in the coming months? How does it look and feel?

Chapter 5

The Awesome Responsibility Involved in Leading Others

Hurdle #5: The Testing of Your Leadership Ability
Without a doubt, your leadership ability will be tested. To clear the hurdle necessary to become an inspirational and impactful leader, you must develop your leadership acumen.

After being interfered with repeatedly by a competing hurdler, I needed to deal with many internal thoughts and feelings and make the necessary adjustments to continue in the race and finish strong as the undisputed winner. Another factor contributing to my decision to remain in the race was that I was the team captain. Many of my teammates were underclassmen, with one or two years remaining in high school. I was a senior preparing to graduate. However, as the team captain, I realized I was a role model in a position of trust and responsibility.

My teammates looked up to me, to be honest, fair, and impartial and treat them as equals. To quit and walk away from my duties would promote team distrust, and I was not about to allow an atmosphere of mistrust to ruin my legacy as an effective team captain. After approaching hurdle five, I had my stride back, and I was settling into my race. My determination to win put me on autopilot.

The Need to be a Trustworthy Leader

As the varsity team captain, how could I let my teammates down by failing to complete a race after being fouled? Furthermore, my coaches and teammates watched me from my sophomore year set an example of leadership and athletic prowess as I led my team as the highest point scorer and Most Valuable Player. **Therefore, as I approached the fifth hurdle in the race, I realized that I needed to settle down and get back into contention because, as the team captain, people were counting on me to perform at my best because they had put their trust in me to demonstrate leadership, even in a pinch.**

Trust is vital for a team captain, a corporate leader, or a homemaker to interact well with their children, teammates, or employees. In addition, trust is critical for leaders to gel with their employees at the corporate level. Fulmer and Gelfand (2012) stated that trust was the linchpin for diverging areas, such as negotiations, team interactions, organizational innovation and change, leadership, and strategic alliances. Pucétaité et al. (2010) argued that organizations that desired to retain committed employees needed to be attentive to their daily operations and procedures, which impacted the employees' experiences and influenced their trust in the organization, as well as their commitment and future with the organization (Vanhala et al., 2016).

Altuntas and Baykal (2010) posited that trust was essential in all organizations, especially staff and management relationships. Moreover, trust was a critical influence that provided the gel that enabled employees to interact collaboratively with those in leadership as they worked together to pursue a common goal. On the other hand, Krot and Lewicka (2012) contended that the trust within an organization between the top administration and their employees took time to establish but could be destroyed relatively quickly, which could spiral to distrust. Therefore, corporate leaders must be aware of the proper development of trust between themselves and their employees while ensuring a milieu of trust between employees who exhibit mutual trust behaviors.

In the literature, organizational trust has many definitions (Krot & Lewicka, 2012). However, for this book, the meaning provided by Cummings and Bromiley (1996) was most appropriate. The two authors provided the following explanation for the concept of organizational trust:

> The belief of an individual or a group of individuals or the organization will make every effort, whether explicit or implied, in good faith to act by commitments; that honesty in relationships will occur because of obligations, and that involved people will not seek to take advantage of others even if they have such opportunities. (p. 303)

Saunders and Thornhill (2004) considered organizational mistrust and distrust to be the opposite of corporate trust. Cho (2006) and Ullmann-Margalit (2004) indicated that distrust did not solely involve the absence of trust; it was a violation of an employee's expectation regarding the reality that their employer would hold their commitment to the welfare and security of the employee. Saunders and Thornhill (2004) suggested that employee mistrust began when employees believed that good behavior and treatment from the employer would not occur due to low mistrust conditions. Saunders and

Thornhill (2004) suggested that employee mistrust began when employees believed that good behavior and treatment from the employer would not occur due to low mistrust conditions.

Mowday et al. (1982) viewed the interactions between the employee and the organizations they associated with as an exchange relationship. Eisenberger et al. (1990) stated that the employee's perception of their exchange relationship with their employer was vital to their commitment to the organization. The authors continued by saying that the perceived organizational support of the employee represented what the organization brought to the exchange equation. The continuous commitment to the organization represented the employee's part of the social exchange relationship.

Blau (1964) contended that while trust was essential in the social exchange process, distrust was also a component of the same interaction. Distrust was at the center of many organizational problems, such as intergroup discard (Insko & Schopler, 1997), reprisal (Bies & Tripp, 1996), and costs associated with conducting business (Levi et al., 2004). While there were many ways to demonstrate social exchange within an organization, the most common exchanges had some standard features. The similarities were

- the initial treatment from an actor to another individual,
- the attitudinal and behavioral responses reciprocated back to the person(s) that initiated the action,
- the formulation of a relationship (Cropanzano et al., 2017).

Are You a Responsible Leader?

Lauer and Blue (n.d.) reported that being named team captain is a distinction of honor. A team honors the person they most respect and trust to lead them to victory. While the designation of the team captain is a great honor, a great responsibility is also associated with the position. Being accountable to one's teammates and coaches is essential for the captain, especially after a bad practice or performance. Even in a clutch, the team captain must continue to compete and lead the team to victory. The team captain must remain in control under pressure while being a role model for their teammates.

Lauer and Blue (n.d.) said that the role of a team captain consists of three Cs: caring, courageousness, and consistency. A caring captain treats their team members with dignity and respect. The team captain focuses on team building as they focus on the well-being of their team members. A team captain must be courageous; that is, they should be able to walk their talk. Team captains exemplify the team's core values, particularly during adverse situations. The team captains are hard workers and hold their teammates to the same work ethic. Lastly, a team captain demonstrates consistency, which entails giving 100% effort during practice and competition.

Leading by example is one way for a person to demonstrate consistency. Some poems emphasize the importance that a leader's lifestyle must support their words, such as the poem listed below:

Hughes, L. "Live Your Creed," in Fonteneau et al., (1996)

The collected poems of Langston Hughes.

World Literature Today, 70(1), 192 wrote

I'd rather see a sermon than to hear one any day.

I'd rather one walk with me than just to show the way.

The eye is a better pupil and more willing than the ear.

Advice may be misleading, but examples are always clear.

And the very best of teachers are the ones who live their creed,

For to see good put into action is what everybody needs.

I can soon learn to do it if you let me see it done.

I can watch your hand in motion but your tongue too fast
may run.

And the lectures you deliver may be very fine and true

But I'd rather get my lesson by observing what you do.

For I may misunderstand you and the fine advice you give

But there's no misunderstanding how you act and how
you live.

When leaders lead by example, they contribute to a cause before requiring involvement from their followers. Thus, leading by example proves to be effective in promoting cooperation while assisting in improving group performance. Moreover, leading by example provides an alternative leadership perspective as it provides a practical way to understand how the group leader influences their followers (Hermalin, 1997).

Since the running of the hurdle race in high school that serves as the basis for this book, my professional career included 15 years as a K-12 site administrator and eight years as a district office administrator, during which I served as the superintendent of schools of a unified school district. Moreover, my church involvement includes serving as senior pastor of a Pentecostal church for more than 30 years, a district superintendent for 21 years, a regional superintendent for the past four years, and a jurisdictional prelate (i.e., bishop) for the past two years.

Also, I have served as the founder and CEO of a nonprofit corporation with an international footprint for the past 21 years. One of the most profound concepts that I learned throughout my many years as a leader was coined by John C. Maxwell, who emphasized the importance of teamwork in his book "Teamwork makes the dream work" (Maxwell, n.d.), which was based on the premise that no great leader can lead alone; instead, great leaders surround themselves with a talented team.

At the age of 65, I fully understand the role of a leader and their need to provide a positive example to their constituency. So let us take a closer look at the leader to become familiar with their function. **Whether on the athletic field or running a multi-million-dollar enterprise, good leadership is the key to the success of any company or athletic team.**

Trainer's Tip #9 – Your leadership acumen can open or close the doors to key opportunities.

One's concept of leadership determines how a leader treats their followers. For example, if leaders view their followers as peons to be manipulated and controlled, they will treat them accordingly. However, if leaders view their followers as essential members of a high-performing team, their behavior will reflect their attitude. One of the most comprehensive explanations of the role of a leader that I embrace and has shaped my understanding regarding the anatomy of an effective leader I derived from Winston and Patterson (2006) in their research entitled, "An Integrative Definition of Leadership."

Following an extensive review of the literature on leadership, the two authors found over 90 variables associated with the understanding of leadership, which they integrated into their definition of leadership. As a result, the two authors defined leadership as follows:

> A leader is one or more people who select, equips, trains, and influences one or more follower(s) who have diverse

gifts, abilities, and skills and focuses the follower(s) on the organization's mission and objectives, causing the follower(s) to expend spiritual, emotional, and physical energy willingly and enthusiastically in a concerted, coordinated effort to achieve the organizational mission and objectives. The leader achieves this influence by humbly conveying a prophetic vision of the future in clear terms that resonate with the follower(s) beliefs and values so that the follower(s) can understand and interpret the end into present-time action steps. In this process, the leader presents the prophetic vision in contrast to the present status of the organization through the use of critical thinking skills, insight, intuition, and the use of both persuasive rhetoric and interpersonal communication, including both active listening and positive discourse, which facilitates and draws forth the opinions and beliefs of the followers such that the followers move through ambiguity toward clarity of understanding to a shared insight that results in influencing the follower(s) to see and accept the future state of the organization as a desirable condition worth committing personal and corporate resources toward its achievement. The leader achieves this using ethical means and seeks the greater good of the follower(s) in the process of action steps such that the follower(s) is/are better off (including the personal development of the follower as well as emotional and physical healing of the follower) because of the interaction with the leader. The leader achieves this same state for his/herself as a leader, as he/she seeks personal growth, renewal, regeneration, and increased stamina–mental, physical, emotional, and spiritual–through the leader-follower interactions. (p. 1)

Your Impact on Others

My role as team captain at the Ventura County Channel League Track and Field Finals was to encourage each participating athlete to represent our high school well, perform at their best ability, exhibit good sportsmanship, and do their part in helping our team to win the league championship. In addition, as team captain and a leader in other venues, I have always sought the best interest of my teammates, followers, employees, and parishioners.

As I lead others, the leadership model that I have employed is transformational leadership (TL). Downton (1973) first espoused TL; then, it became popularized as a theory by Burns (1978). TL moved away from viewing leaders by their traits, personalities, and transactions to their ability to build up others to reach their highest degree of potential.

Bass and Bass (2008) reported that the transformational leader could encourage and influence followers to go beyond self-centeredness to positively impact the group, corporation, or humanity. In addition, transformational leaders elevate the followers' concerns to issues of success.

The three key characteristics that depict TL are as follows:

1. The transformational leader offers encouragement and motivation to the follower.

2. The transformational leader works for the mutual good of the follower; and

3. The transformational leader is a change agent (Bagram & Altaf, 2009; Givens, 2008).

Transformational leaders are concerned with their followers' development as they inspire them to engage in noteworthy endeavors. TL stresses that leaders acknowledge and adjust to the wants and drives of followers. Transformational leaders are agents of change who are reputable role models, who build and publicize a precise concept for an organization, and who stimulates followers to meet higher standards, which function in a way that influences others to trust them, and who offer meaning to organizational endeavors (Northouse, 2019).

As you read this book, you may not see yourself as a role model. For example, you may not be involved in athletics or run a corporation; nonetheless, someone is always watching your life. Will you be an example for others to emulate, or will you live capriciously and arbitrarily, not recognizing the level of influence that you may have on another person?

When my daughter Olympia was a senior in high school, she also participated in track and field. One day, while we were at church, a lady approached my daughter and stated that her child wanted to grow up and become the same kind of athlete as my daughter. This young girl wrote my daughter a letter and drew a picture of her participating in the long jump event. During her sophomore year in high school, Olympia set a school and meet record in the long jump as she competed against a field of good competitors.

Olympia was surprised that she was a role model for this little girl because she did not know her. That is the reason that I contend that someone is always watching you. Therefore, whether you are a homemaker, a gardener, or a caretaker, you never know how you will positively and negatively influence others, so always be on your best behavior.

I understood the job I needed to do to win the 120-yard high hurdle race, so I told myself, "Feet, don't fail me now." Then, like in the novel Forrest Gump (Winston, 1986), when a group of bullies was chasing young Forrest, a young girl encouraged him to escape by yelling, "Run, Forrest, Run!" I reached deep down inside and garnered the courage to win. Can you envision yourself going within and stirring up the motivation and encouragement needed to overcome your dilemma? I know you can. I am counting on you to emerge as an overcomer.

The Mindset of an Overcomer

Overcomers understand that leaders are in a position of trust; therefore, leadership is a calling that should be handled with diligence, finesse, and dedication.

Reflective Questions

1. Do you consider yourself a leader? If not, why not?

2. Do you have a level of influence over someone? If so, identify that person and prepare notes regarding your accountability to them.

3. What type of leadership style do you use? If you do not know, research different leadership theories and models, and identify your preferred style.

4. Reread the comprehensive function of the role of a leader above. Were you able to identify with any of the presented behaviors? If not, do your research on the life of a leader that greatly influenced others.

5. Do you have the tenacity of a Forrest Gump to run out of the chains and bondages you currently face during your season of adversity? If so, identify a strategy that will help you overcome your dilemma.

Chapter 6

Regaining the Lead

Hurdle #6: Your Lead Will be Challenged
Failing to remain focused after losing your lead in a competition can compromise your ability to regain the lead.

Coming from behind in a race after losing the lead can become a daunting task that requires a different mindset than a runner who takes an early lead and remains out front or a runner who never had the lead and comes from behind to win at the end of a competition. **Having something and losing it, then trying to regain what was lost, can become overwhelming.** Therefore, I like movies that are adventures involving lost treasure. In some films, the protagonist and his team fight terrible odds searching for treasure or a priceless artifact. The nerve-shaking part of the movie consists of a nemesis, who, searching for the same priceless treasure(s), follows the film's star and confiscates the treasure(s). Once the protagonist learns that an enemy stole their prize, their heart sinks into despair because the cost of refinancing their project to locate and retrieve their valued item sometimes involves large sums of money.

So, to think about the reality of reclaiming something that was once in an individual's possession can be overwhelming. However, the person who maintains a never-give-up, never-quit attitude becomes a formidable foe who will stop at nothing to recover what belongs to them. Thus, the described scenario embodies the philosophy advocated in this book.

After reaching hurdle six, I prepared to pass the two remaining hurdlers temporarily in the lead to regain the lead once again. My adrenaline level was running high as I approached these two competitors, not because of fear but because of the excitement associated with making a successful comeback. Not only did I have the courage necessary to challenge their lead and overtake them, but I was also unwilling to allow them to take away something that I knew was mine. I remained undefeated during all regular league races in the 120-yard high hurdle and the 330-yard low hurdle races but was defeated during some of the invitational meet races. With the reality of my undefeated status in the league, I was unwilling to allow another competitor to receive the league championship medal that represented the crowning glory of a successful track season and the recognition of a job well done.

Trainer's Tip #10 – Never allow someone to take the lead you once had without putting up a fierce fight to regain it.

Regaining the Lead

Have you ever been fired from a job without cause, lost your home in foreclosure, or suffered a painful divorce? If so, you understand the devastation of loss and the long road of recovery ahead if you choose not to give up and quit. Sometimes the financial repercussions can become too difficult to handle. Unfortunately, many people who have suffered significant losses decide to give up, which only complicates their problem(s).

In an article entitled, "How to Mentally Recover After a Financial Setback," Karimi (2017) reported that a severe financial setback should not lead to a personal meltdown in an individual's life. Instead, rebounding from the devastating impact of financial loss is possible if the impacted person remains sensible and commits to creating a long-term strategy for an economic comeback. The seven practical steps involved in the financial recovery process are as follows:

1. Do not overreact by utilizing an emotional, knee-jerk reaction. Instead, take a realistic view of your situation and seek practical solutions contributing to long-term recovery.

2. Find a trusted family member, friend, or support group to provide emotional support during the crisis.

3. Take time to perform a realistic assessment of the loss incurred, no matter the emotional toll of conducting the inventory, and develop a plan conducive to financial recovery.

4. Revisit your monthly budget to reprioritize past priorities to reflect the reality of the present situation. Doing so can free up the resources necessary to increase your cash flow.

5. Take care of yourself by not engaging in unhealthy behaviors such as drinking alcohol, eating junk foods, and not exercising. Instead, be sure to get adequate rest or try developing a healthy fitness plan, to name a few.

6. Do not beat yourself up by becoming overly critical of your mistake; remember that everyone makes mistakes.

7. Create a new vision to pursue based on your current reality and move into the future with new financial goals (Karimi, 2017, paras 1-7).

Yes, the losses you incur when faced with adversity may result in a temporary setback; moving forward or remaining where you are is up to you. Rebranding your image, rebuilding your business, and entering a new relationship await those not afraid to move forward in life.

What Will You Do After Losing Everything?

In his presentation at TEDxLancasterU, entitled "Losing Everything is the Perfect Opportunity," Arash Aazami (2015) discussed his story as a White child raised in a small West African village. After leaving Africa when he was grown, he returned to his country of origin, the Netherlands, where he began studying to play the electric guitar at a conservatory. Life was good for Aazami until he lost his job, wife, finances, and home. Although Aazami experienced personal losses, he still felt empowered to improve as a person and live life at its best, not allowing his setback to get the best of him. Even though all he possessed was lost, Aazami still believed he could do anything he set his mind to do.

While unemployed, Aazami (2015) was very selective in the employment opportunities that he sought after. He was not interested in securing employment that just paid well; he wanted his work to be meaningful, purpose-driven, and fulfilling. Ultimately, he purchased an energy company to establish its direction. His company became very successful. In a time of self-reflection, Aazami wondered how his life shifted from playing the electric guitar to becoming the owner of an electric company. He concluded that by saying "no" to so many job offers, he was empowered to say "yes" to the right opportunity, which involved leading an energy company. He was now the owner of a company. However, the company was in bad shape as it suffered from poor sales and unmotivated employees.

Despite all the challenges, Aazami accepted the leadership position for the failing company. While he knew nothing about energy, yet he knew much about how people thought and behaved. After questioning many of the staff at the energy company, he learned that they had lost the concept of what the company was selling energy. He asked about sustainability, consumption, and sales. Aazami found that their assumptions were faulty at best. Realizing that the world was running out of fossil fuel-based energy resources, he felt the company should transition into sustainable and renewable energy resources. Aazami wanted his company to maintain a worldwide perspective of sustainable energy because millions of people depended upon energy. Ultimately, he created a new sustainable energy model by conceiving an idea of an energy company that would earn more money by selling less energy.

This concept sounded impossible, but Aazami believed that his idea would work. Hence, he quit his former job and pursued his new venture. Aazami stated that he thought a company should be a means to an end and not serve as the end, as in most traditional models. Therefore, he desired to serve the end. To do so, he needed to know what the end entailed, and as a result, Aazami returned to the small village in Africa where he grew up in search of an answer. He found that while the school he attended in Africa did not have electricity, it had "vintage" Microsoft Excel. In addition, many Africans who lived in the village had cellular phones despite no electricity.

He also found that the people recharged their cell phones using a diesel engine-powered generator.

Upon his return, Aazami brought a suitcase full of solar-powered lights and phone chargers, which he distributed among the village's children. His concern for the well-being of the children involved them in becoming the leaders of the future who needed an energy source to power lights for them to continue their studies once the sun went down. The power from renewable energy sources would enhance the quality of their educational experience, which would only contribute to them experiencing a brighter future. Aazami did not want to give away the lights powered by renewable energy for free; however, he required all students receiving his equipment to agree to plant a tree and nurture it until maturity as payment. Today, the mobile network in that small village is powered by solar energy derived from solar panels and streetlights powered by sunlight. Aazami believed that energy is a basic need that all people should have. Therefore, Aazami wanted to see energy categorized as a fundamental human right available to all regardless of economic status (Aazami, 2015).

After I listened to the story of Aazami and learned of the bad breaks he encountered in his marriage and career, it is a wonder that he did not throw in the towel and quit. He realized, however, that his life entailed greater meaning than the trials he had experienced, and ultimately, he was not afraid to pick up where he left off and move on to have a brighter future. In your situation, you can learn from the example of Aazami and set your sights on a brighter future.

You may have suffered great trials like Aazami and found that you have lost everything. There is nothing positive about suffering significant loss. However, despite your situation, you can always recalibrate the direction of your life to pursue loftier goals that may even involve improving the lives of millions of people worldwide, just like him. A poem entitled "See It Through" highlights the process that a person may go through after suffering great adversity and loss. Seeing things through to the end leads to many possibilities that a person could experience on the other side of not giving up. The poem reads as follows:

When you're up against a trouble,

Meet it squarely, face to face;

Lift your chin and set your shoulders,

Plant your feet and take a brace.

When it's vain to try to dodge it,

Do the best that you can do;

You may fail, but you may conquer,

See it through!

Black may be the clouds about you

And your future may seem grim,

But don't let your nerve desert you;

Keep yourself in fighting trim.

If the worst is bound to happen,

In spite of all that you can do,

Running from it will not save you,

See it through!

Even hope may seem but futile,

When with troubles you're beset,

But remember you are facing

Just what other men have met.

You may fail, but fall still fighting;

Don't give up, whate'er you do;

Eyes front, head high to the finish.

See it Through. (Edgar A. Guest, 2007, para 1)

I often talk to my youngest daughter, Jennifer, about her job as a private school administrator after she becomes frustrated over a troubling situation. From her perspective, those situations can seem all-consuming. As we tackle the problem together, I draw upon my past career as a public school administrator and help her analyze the problem and develop alternative strategies that she may not have considered. At the end of our sessions, she looks at me like I am a genius. However, like the poem stated above, the issues related to my daughter's profession are commonplace, and other administrators have faced them in the past and found success. Therefore, I advise her to maintain the fortitude and tenacity to deal with the problem until we find an amicable solution.

Keep Your Eyes on the Prize

In my upbringing in a Pentecostal denomination, I would hear the old saints of God sing a song that contained the following lyrics: "Lord, I'm striving, trying to make a hundred; ninety-nine and a half won't do" (Gospel Nostalgia, 2012). The song's sentiments emanated from the hearts of people who had their eyes set on

Heaven as their eternal reward for their belief in Jesus Christ and their corresponding lifestyle on their pilgrimage journey to Heaven–their eternal destiny.

The song demonstrated that their ultimate objective was to meet Jesus face to face and live with Him eternally. However, in doing so, they understood the reality of setting earthly goals worthy of receiving the Lord's approval in the end. Therefore, living a compromising lifestyle that sometimes would involve behaviors that displeased the Lord was unacceptable.

After passing the final two leaders of the hurdle race, I had retaken the lead, reaching an immediate goal of coming from behind to regain the lead; however, taking the lead was only a part of my greater objective, which was to win the race. Some people in my predicament would have been pleased to catch those in the lead and would have stopped short of their intended aim to win the race. They would have allowed their primary objective to be subverted by settling for fulfilling a short-term goal.

Williams (2012) purported that one way for a person to reach their intended objective involves setting SMART goals–goals that are specific, measurable, attainable, realistic, and timely. Individuals who develop a specific purpose know what they intend to accomplish. Measurability involves establishing a number to measure completion. Attainability allows one to determine whether one can reach their goal. Knowing that a plan is doable entails being realistic. Moreover, understanding the amount of time involved in attaining a dream is essential for goal setting.

Jeffery Davis (1996), in his book, *Managing and Achieving Organizational Goals,* contended that, in the corporate arena, goal setting is paramount to the success of any enterprise. He wrote that goal setting was an important tool that organizations used to establish their goals and the direction of their companies. Establishing long-term and short-term goals assists in the following areas:

- improved product quality
- greater customer focus
- improved customer relations
- reduction of errors.

In 1942, an investment company called Babson's Report modified Benjamin Franklin's famous saying, "For us to fail to prepare, is to prepare to fail," changing it to "If you fail to plan, you are planning to fail." The company understood the power of planning for those who intended to invest their money and expected a bountiful yield in return (Franklin et al., 2018).

It is time for you to remember that while you still have breath in your lungs, the will to move forward, and the right mindset, your life is not over. I understand your loss and the devastation that followed your adversity. No one likes to lose. No one likes having the wind knocked out of them during life episodes. However, nothing can stop you from dreaming again.

You may have lost everything important to you, including your family, friends, job, and finances. Although your loss may have been significant, you can still change the trajectory of your life in positive ways. By not giving up, caving in, and quitting, you can plan for a brighter future that entails global proportions. It is time for you to get back in the game and refocus your attention on a destination with your destiny written all over it.

Remember, destiny calls. Before David became the King of Judah and Israel, he experienced a great defeat as he and his men returned from battle to find that the enemy had raided their hometown and stolen their families and possessions; so, David had to encourage himself and depend on God to regain what was lost. David and his soldiers recovered everything they initially lost, and he became the second King of Israel and a man after God's own heart (*King James Bible*, 1769/2017, 1 Sam.1-31).

The Mindset of an Overcomer

Overcomers understand that there is still life after they have suffered loss, so they strive to make the best of a bad situation.

Reflective Questions

1. Have you counted yourself out in life after facing adversity? Why?

2. Do you not realize that the same God that enabled you to achieve all that you lost is still able to direct your life to a brighter future? Think about this, then ask God for help.

3. Have you taken inventory of your many positive qualities? If not, then do so. If you have, then it is time to put them to use.

4. Have you established your S.M.A.R.T. goals? If not, start planning.

5. What do you plan to accomplish within the next year, the next five years, and ten years from now? You can make things happen with the help of God, a positive attitude, and a committed spirit.

Chapter 7

No Time to Rest on Past Laurels

Hurdle #7: Reliance Upon Past Successes to Resolve New Challenges
Resist the temptation to rest on past success(es) because your past success(es) is only helpful if you use the information you gained in it to face the new set of challenges you will undoubtedly face in all your future races.

This book centers on a race I experienced in 1975 while participating in the Ventura County Channel League Track and Field Finals. I overcame outside interference from another competitor, who compromised my anticipated victory. Yes, while competing in other important hurdle races early in the season, there were times that the interference was of my own making after I stiffened up during races, which resulted in me hitting hurdles causing me to lose those races. In this particular race, the interference resulted as a competitor spiked me over the first and second hurdles, which threw me out of contention for the lead in the race. However, after deciding not to quit, I remained in the race, determined to regain the lead and win.

As I approached hurdle seven, I was now in a comfortable lead, accelerating rapidly ahead of the other competitors. However, I realized that if I wanted to win the race, I could not revert to the behavior that caused me to stiffen up and hit hurdles. By doing so, I would compromise the remainder of the race. So, I ran harder than ever before between each remaining hurdle, and as I should, like I had trained hard to do, I remained relaxed in the process.

This problem of tightening up during a race did not start in high school. It began years before. My 6th-grade teacher would have our class compete in the 50-yard dash when I was in elementary school. I liked the race and ran it very well. However, I learned some destructive behaviors that would affect me for many years. I noticed that when most of the boys ran, they would bend their heads back, grit their teeth with grimacing looks on their faces, and ball up their hands in a fist to run faster. So, I adapted to their behavior, thinking that the tighter I ran, the faster I would go.

Because I was naturally fast, the adverse effects of tightening up during the race did not impact me as I beat my competitors. However, when I reached my senior year in high school, I learned that when I tightened up while running the hurdles, I would hit some of the barriers resulting in me running slower races. I did not realize that running tight contracted my muscles, causing them not to extend to their maximal range. The antithesis of running tight was running relaxed.

It was not until I went to college and began participating in collegiate sports that I fully understood the impact that running tight or relaxed had on a sprinter or hurdler. At UCR, my coach taught me the benefits of running and remaining relaxed throughout the race to maximize my muscle range. He explained that I could determine whether I was running tight or relaxed by placing my thumb on my pointing finger during practice runs. As my thumb put more pressure on my pointing finger, it indicated that I was running too tightly. In contrast, if my thumb rested on my pointing finger without undue pressure, it revealed that I was running loose and relaxed. Therefore, I realized that when an athlete tightens up during a race, the strain negatively impacts their performance. Although there are other factors involved, all things being equal, the athlete that runs relaxed will end up the victor.

While in high school, the April rains hindered our team from practicing outside. The wet conditions placed a temporary moratorium on our track and field competition participation. However, the break was a blessing in disguise. It provided me with a brief hiatus from the competition gruel and gave me time to stretch, soak in the Jacuzzi, and relax my mind. Doing so allowed me to run relaxed while participating in the upcoming Ventura County Channel League Track and Field Finals.

New Problems Entail New Solutions

In the business arena, researchers discovered that an inappropriate response to the demands associated with changing times within their environments led large companies to fail. The problems these companies experienced emanated from competitors bringing in new products, strategies, and technologies that rivaled and eclipsed their business. Unable to compete, sales dwindled, and their enterprises suffered financially. The decline in sales ultimately led to these organizations' demise. When faced with changing times and new competitors, management must develop new perspectives and employ new strategies. Unfortunately, amid a climate of challenge and adversity, some companies allow their loyalty to the past to overshadow reason. They reverted to old practices that brought them past success and paid a high price for their inappropriate response to change.

Most managers assume that paralysis is the number one problem that causes organizations to fail during troubled times because paralysis involves leadership freezing in their tracks when confronting adversity. However, identifying paralysis as the culprit proved to be an incorrect assessment because, in most cases, the management of the embattled enterprise maintained an early recognition of the threat to their company and responded to it with a battery of initiatives to no avail. Many times, stubbornness on the part of those in leadership was a factor that impacted their company's demise, and the most common reason involved active inertia. Some physicists contend that inertia happens when a moving object maintains its current trajectory without wavering off course. Thus, active inertia in an organizational setting involves relying on established behavior patterns even after a substantial shift within its environment. Therefore, depending on old-fashioned responses that brought an organization prominence in the past only exacerbated the problem by dragging the company further and further down (Sull, 1999).

While serving as a school administrator, I was amazed at the number of school districts that ended up in program improvement, districts that, at one time, had operated at the epitome of pedagogy. However, over time these districts experienced a change in their demographics, which brought in a new group of students with different educational problems and unique needs, e.g., the English Language Learner population and students of lower social and economic status. In response to these school districts' new needs and demands, their administrators relied on programs and plans that had once brought them success. However, the problems they faced fundamentally differed from anything they had experienced. As a result, despite good intentions and reasonable efforts, these districts could not appropriately educate their new students.

Consequently, they were placed on program improvement status and faced the imminent takeover of their districts by an administrator assigned by the California State Department of Education. These once-thriving school districts faced academic failure and the threat of a state takeover because they did not perform their due diligence in properly identifying their challenges and current state, which included an understanding of the unique needs that emerged as the districts' demographics changed. Therefore, as the district administrators sought to address their educational predicaments, they sought to fix their problems with antiquated solutions that did not work for their new students. As you would guess, their dilemma worsened as time passed, and many of these schools were forced to contend with being subordinated to a state administrator. Go-Deskless (2020) provided further insight into why the mentioned school districts ended up in program improvement, i.e., they may have responded to the external threat; nonetheless, their strategy was inappropriate.

The following is a powerful example of how an organization can remain competitive by staying ahead of the curb. An analysis of the Toyota corporation that investigated its strengths and weaknesses to understand its dominance in the automotive industry found that Toyota has remained competitive globally due to its commitment to research and development (R&D). Through an aggressive R&D focus, Toyota seeks to expand its product portfolio. Also, Toyota aims to improve its product's functionality, quality, safety, and environmental abilities. Through R&D, Toyota continues to enhance the capabilities of its current products by improving them while also developing new products prepared for future markets. Because of Toyota's commitment to R&D, it remains dominant in technological leadership over its global competitors. In addition, because Toyota leads the market in innovative products, the company benefits from solid sales (Nkomo, 2013).

From my perspective, Toyota understood what it took to gain ground over its competitors and remain in the lead. Through Toyota's dependence on an aggressive R&D approach, it secured its position as one of the world's top automotive makers and distributors. Similarly, in assessing my position in the race at the sixth and seventh hurdles, I chose not to believe that I could not improve my performance. So, I ran faster, attacked the hurdles more aggressively, and ran like my life depended on

it. Employing the stated strategy assisted me in remaining out front.

Trainer's Tip #11 – To remain competitive, you must become a lifelong learner–one who is open to personal improvement and one who embraces change.

An organization's management can avoid the adverse effects of active inertia within their enterprise once they understand its sources and symptoms. For example, if the administration believes that the culprit leading to the demise of their business is paralysis, they will engage in fruitless actions; however, if they understand that taking extreme action could become the enemy, they will take a deeper look into their assumptions before proceeding forward. As they look deeper into their efforts, they may gain a clearer perspective of their responses to the problem. Doing so will minimize the odds of falling into the same trap as other fallen leaders (Sull, 1999).

Now Is Not the Time for Slacking

While playing football for Ventura High School during my sophomore year, our team played against Santa Clara High School in Oxnard, CA. The stats favored us to win the game because we were in a larger CIF division four school, and Santa Clara High School was in a different division for small schools. We played a scrimmage game against Santa Clara High School that did not count towards our league standing. We dominated the game in the first quarter. By halftime, the score was 21 to 7, favoring Ventura. Our head coach was so happy with our performance that he allowed our team to relax and tank up on water at halftime. One of the assistant coaches tried to reason with the head coach not to let our team slack off during halftime but to no avail. Our head coach believed our game domination would continue into the second half. Therefore, after halftime, the head coach replaced the starting first-team players and allowed the second and third-string players to start. To our surprise and chagrin, Santa Clara High School beat our team after halftime, 24 to 21. Yes, we were a better team; however, our coaches' assessment that we were the dominant team caused him to have a lapse in judgment, let down his guard, and subsequently, we lost the game.

When running a ballistic race such as the 100-meter dash or 110-high hurdle race, if a runner looks around to see their competitors' position, they may lose their leading position by hitting a hurdle and causing them to stumble or fall, which could negatively influence their race. Now that I was in a comfortable lead, I realized that the runners I passed were still viable competitors in the race. At that moment, I could only assume that one of them was behind me, plotting to overtake me again for the lead, but I did not look around. Instead, I kept my focus on the goal ahead of me.

In business, competition is paramount on a global scale. Because of the realities of other competitors striving to either take the lead or remain in the lead to dominate a particular market, the organizations that plan to be competitive and stay relevant in a specific market develop strategic plans. Moreover, another important activity that an organization takes to remain in the lead of its competitors is to undertake a competitor or competitive analysis (Adom et al., 2016). Zahra and Chaples (1993) defined *competitive analysis* as a process that a company employs to learn and comprehend its industry's competitors to estimate its rival's strengths and weaknesses while anticipating their moves. Conducting a competitor or competitive analysis allows an organization to determine its position among its rivals (Adom et al., 2016). While it is essential to understand a competitor's threat, do not overestimate your competitor or underestimate your potential. Yes, we all compete in various areas of our lives. All competition is not sports-related. It may be the competition you face in seeking promotion or something else. We should all understand the truth behind what motivates our rivals–they want what is ours or do not want to lose what is theirs.

The *Holy Bible* provides an example of the negative consequences of forgetting who God is and who we are in relationship to Him. God directed Moses to send a group of spies out on a reconnaissance mission to survey the land of Canaan–a piece of land that He had promised to give Israel. Unfortunately, they underestimated the military prowess that came from their dependence on the LORD of Hosts and overestimated their foe's supposed military might. While Israel had the promise of God that He was with them and the land was theirs to possess, Israel still needed to fight and take possession of their property because other nations currently occupied the land. Ten of the twelve spies who surveyed Canaan returned with the negative report that they could not take the territory because their competitors were so tall that they viewed themselves as grasshoppers. Conversely, two spies returned with a positive message acknowledging that, while there were giants in the land, they could defeat them in battle (*New King James Bible*, 2004, Numbers.13:1-3, 17-20, 23-33).

Too many times, we become our worst enemies because of our fears, inferiorities, and "stinking thinking." Unlike how Israel reacted to the giants that occupied the land they were to possess, we should face our giants with God-inspired courage. We must realize that we are not in the battle alone. We have a mighty God who promises to fight on our behalf because there is more to the land set before us than the threat of giant people. The Israelites should have remembered that God told them that He had already given them the land. They only needed to take possession. The Israelites should have given greater consideration to the fact that the land was fertile and produced fruit so large that it took two men to carry a cluster of grapes. Moreover, the pomegranates and figs were also massive. After eating manna (i.e., edible food that God provided from Heaven) for nearly forty years while they wandered through the desert, Israel should have been ecstatic to discover a place with the bounty of food that the land of Canaan possessed.

Why not take a fresh look at the opposition you once faced or currently face through a lens of optimism to reassess their threat level? For example, in 1974, Muhammed Ali fought George Foreman in a fight in Zaire, Africa, billed as "The Rumble in the Jungle." Ali was once the undisputed heavyweight boxing champion of the world. However, in response to his refusal to be inducted into the armed forces during the Vietnam war due to his religious convictions, the boxing commission stripped Ali of his championship title. As a result, Ali sat out from boxing for approximately four years before resuming his boxing career. At 32 years of age, after having his championship belt removed a few years earlier, Ali entered the fight as a four-to-one underdog to the virile George Foreman. The latter, at age 25, was the world's undisputed champion. In preparation for the contest, Ali developed a strategy called the "rope-a-dope" as he considered Foreman's strength and punching ability. Ali's plan involved allowing George Foreman to punch himself out until he was tired. In the eighth round of the fight, Ali knocked out Foreman in a stunning victory and regained his title as the world's undisputed heavyweight champion boxer. Later, Ali became known as the greatest (Wikipedia, 2021). With God, no matter your age or circumstances, you, too, can make a stunning comeback.

Never Underestimate Your Potential

As previously stated, if you overestimate your competitor's potential and underestimate your own, there are ensuing consequences. The consequences could be devastating, ranging from causing you to lose your race or organizational advantage, demoralizing your employees, and compromising the growth and success of your organization. For example, let us take a closer look at the negative report from ten of the twelve spies after they surveyed the land of Canaan. The negative news they brought back was so dismal that it demoralized Israel and caused them to become afraid of the inhabitants that possessed the land and refuse to enter Canaan as God had commanded.

The book of Numbers offers a closer look into the children of Israel's behavior and subsequent consequences for their disobedience and unbelief (*New King James Bible*, 2004, Numbers 14:1-10, 20-24). After hearing the report of the twelve spies, the Israelites accepted the negative assessment that came from the ten spies and rejected the positive message of the two spies. The verdict was to cut bait and run. In actuality, the Israelites became so fearful of their perceived impending fate that they considered harming Moses and the two spies that provided a favorable report. However, through the grace of God, the Israelites did not follow through with harming these three men.

Israel's assessment of its inability to fight and conquer the land over the current occupants was erroneous. Biblical history proves that Israel's fears regarding the giants were inaccurate as the giants feared the Israelites even more. The book of Joshua records an account of a situation that happened after the death of Moses. Joshua, one of the spies that provided a favorable report and was now the leader of the Israelites, sent two spies once again to spy out the land of Canaan, particularly the city of Jericho. The two spies stayed with a lady named Rahab, a prostitute, that hid the spies and allowed them to stay in her house for a while. During her conversation with the spies, she stated that she understood that the Lord had given the land of Canaan to the Children of Israel. She announced that all the inhabitants of the city, who were the same giants that the ten spies feared, became faint-hearted when they heard that the Israelites were preparing to invade their land. When the giants heard how the Lord had opened the Red Sea for the Israelites after they left Egypt and considered that they had destroyed any enemy that stood against them, their hearts melted with fear (*New King James Bible*, 2004, Joshua.1:1-18). **The moral of this Biblical story is never to overestimate your enemies' ability or underestimate your potential because your assessment may be inaccurate. The loss you face from not engaging may be worse than what you feared engaging.** Also, it is better to fight and potentially lose than to experience the emotional and spiritual deficit that comes with not fighting a battle God directs you to fight. Israel gave us an example of what can happen to those who discount the power of God and themselves. God did intervene, but He prevented the children of Israel from entering Canaan–the Promise Land that He had promised them.

Have you allowed negative thoughts or influences to invade your mind, causing you to negatively assess your potential as you move forward? Early in life, I learned it is hard to move forward looking in the rear-view mirror. Whether your future is bright, rosy, or full of gloom is in your hands. Your past, no matter how difficult, is behind you. Your future lies ahead. Yes, I know God is in ultimate control of your life, but you are required to give him something in which to work. Since what I just stated is true, why not put your best foot forward and give God your best? Remember what the Apostle Paul admonished all believers to know about God's tremendous power. Paul made the following declaration found in the book of Ephesians 3:20 (*New King James Version*, 1982), which reads as follows: "Now to Him who is able to do exceedingly abundantly above all that we ask or think, according to the power that works in us."

The Mindset of an Overcomer

Overcomers understand that it takes hard work to accomplish anything in life, especially to recover from a loss. Therefore, there is never time for complacency.

Reflective Questions

1. Have you allowed yourself to become immobilized following adversity? Why?

2. Do you think it is time to throw in the towel and quit? Why?

3. Have you taken an inventory of your assets and weaknesses? If so, how will you use your assets to your advantage and strengthen or eliminate your weaknesses? Make a plan.

4. Do you believe now is the time to get back in the race and take control of your destiny? If so, or if not, why?

5. Will you take the time to read and meditate on Ephesians 3: 20 and learn what God has in store for your future?

Chapter 8

Becoming an Incompatible Force

Hurdle #8: Overcoming the Battle of Life
You will face your battle of life. Win it, and the world will swing wide its doors to you. Lose it, and the world will shut you out of a lifetime of opportunities that were designed for you. Therefore, fight to win at all costs; your future depends on it.

When I ran track and field for UCR, an older gentleman named Jason would join our team during practice. He was a sprinter. Jason was a realist because he knew he was not fast enough to beat any of our sprinters. Still, Jason was keenly aware that during practice, if any one of us were to make a mistake while running, such as slipping, tightening up, or falling, he would be close enough to capitalize on our misfortune. Playfully, in a gentle taunt before each practice activity, such as running a 330-yard sprint, he would warn us, "Don't slip because I will beat you!"

Although this elderly gentleman was 20-30 years our senior and could not have beaten us outright, he was fast enough to remain near the pack. He trained with us to continue his domination in the senior leagues, where he competed in track and field. None of us wanted to be this older man's first victim. So, to maintain our dignity, we ran our best to exert our dominant force over him as younger collegiate athletes when he trained with us.

Returning my attention to the 1975 Ventura County Channel League Track and Field Finals, I was in a comfortable lead in the 120-yard high hurdle race as I cleared the eighth hurdle. Nonetheless, I had to focus on my goals: run fast, run hard, and finish first. You see, my destiny lay ahead. The CIF Division Four Prelims and Finals were just days away, and I wanted to be one of the few runners in Southern California to participate in that competition. Therefore, despite being comfortably in the lead, I had to set my focus forward. I could not rely on past successes and accomplishments which were responsible for me being in that enviable position.

Do not Allow Your Competitors to Overtake You

To ensure that my current position in the race was on task to reach my goals and objectives, I mentally conducted a brief personal performance management (PM) and performance appraisal (PA) assessment to check my status. In the business world, PMs are part of the assessment process that provides vital feedback to the leadership of an organization, while PAs provide annual assessments of the performances of their employees. PM involves a goal-oriented process developed to ensure that organizational processes and activities maximize employees, teams, and productivity. PM establishes the measurement and improvement of the workforce. Through PM, incentive goals and corresponding values become communicated to be understood by all employees of an organization. Thus, a close association between performance and incentives exists because as the performance of an employee increases, so does the incentive. Each part of an organizational system includes performance management measures such as training, appraisal, and rewards to maximize continuous organizational effectiveness. If the PM indicates a need to improve a worker's skill(s), measures are implemented to provide training as needed. Through the PM systems, training becomes connected to attaining organizational effectiveness. By ignoring PM, an organization invites failure. Therefore, an organization must integrate its mission and vision into its performance management system to achieve maximal success (Gillen, 2007). On the other hand, performance appraisal (PA) is the process of employee performance on an ongoing basis. PA involves assessing employee performance over time (SHRM, 2010).

As a high school athlete, I regularly received PM and PA assessments to determine if I was on target in meeting team goals and performing at a level established by the head coach. My high school coach provided valuable feedback regarding my performance during or immediately following a competition. He would address those areas identified as needing improvement with an action plan to correct the deficit(s). Conversely, I would receive my coach's approval if my performance met his standard. I found the feedback vital as it allowed me to adjust when necessary. So, I conducted a self-assessment to rate my overall performance in a brief second. I could once again hear the crowd's roar as I moved closer to the finish line. Some of my teammates positioned near the last three hurdles yelled, "Go, Gabriel!" Knowing that the adversity I faced earlier in the race was over, my stride running between the hurdles became swifter, and I felt strong. I was relaxed but running with great determination. The feedback from the self-assessment indicated that I was on target to reach my main objective, i.e., win the race and take home the league medal.

Overcoming the Battle of Life

Trainer's Tip #12 – Everyone must confront and overcome their battle of life.

When I was a young man, in a teachable moment, my mother taught me the importance of overcoming the battle of life. She defined the battle of life as the process every person alive must undergo, such as experiencing misfortunes, adversities, and setbacks. She believed that if a person overcame their challenges in life, they would position themselves to achieve their life's destiny. However, if a person failed their life's test, they would become less than their destiny intended. Therefore, I now share my mother's teachable moment with you. You must confront and overcome your battle of life before you can reach your life's destiny.

In Ventura, CA, during the 1960s, one of the town bums (i.e., town drunk) was named Tex. Unfortunately, Tex was an alcoholic who lived for the next drink. Nonetheless, Tex was a gentle person who would not hurt a fly. I remember the times on the weekend when I would see Tex exiting the corner liquor store. If he observed my brother Michael and me coming his way, he would stop us and beckon us to the store counter, where they kept the penny candies. A penny could purchase up to three small candies back in those days. Tex would pay the penny to buy my brother and me the candy.

I would ask my mother about the circumstances that led to Tex's misfortune. My mother would reply that he had lost his battle of life. Therefore, his present state resulted from him giving up on life. I did not fully understand what my mother conveyed until I was much older and after I went through several battles of my own. Fortunately, in keeping with my mother's advice, I faced each of my struggles and conquered them.

Now that I am in my 60s, I recognize that my younger self, who was in the lead of the 120-yard high hurdle race, learned the importance of overcoming adversity to achieve desired goals and objectives. This determination propelled me to win at all costs and not to become distracted, disappointed, or disillusioned, and in the process provided me with the tools to overcome any difficulty I may face in this life.

As a result of learning how to overcome in life, I have remained married for over 40 years to the young lady who sat in the grandstands, cheering me on. Together we raised three lovely daughters, each of whom earned advanced degrees in college. We are now the proud grandparents of seven grandchildren, with a great-grandchild on the way. I could go on and on about the blessings my wife and I are now experiencing in life. Many of our blessings would not be possible if I had responded to challenging trials by quitting and blaming others early on. Reflecting back, I can see that the lessons I learned by remaining in the race have guided me through life. I am so grateful that God enabled me to overcome my challenges and win the battle of life.

You, too, most certainly have experienced many battles throughout your lifetime. How did you handle them? Did you stand up and fight, or did you allow your struggle to get the best of you? Going forward, you will experience failure in some of your battles, but do not dismay or be filled with anxiety. There is yet hope because you are still alive. Yes, the process will be challenging and even scary, but you still have a chance to be an overcomer.

After reading this book, implement the principles you have learned to give yourself the determination and desire to win again. Nothing is impossible for you to achieve with the Lord on your side. So, I admonish you to get back in the game and pursue your destiny with renewed vigor. Your life depends on it!

The *Holy Bible* reveals that the Apostle Paul understood the importance of not allowing his negative past to hinder his progress in his new life. For those among my readers who are not familiar with Paul, here is a peek into his background. Prior to his conversion Paul, formerly known as Saul, achieved the status of a Pharisee; he sat as a member of the Sanhedrin Court, a highly exalted position of authority. In his zeal to protect his Jewish faith, Paul abused and tormented Jews that converted to Christianity. While on his way to Damascus to persecute Christians, Jesus confronted Saul about his behavior, which led to his conversion to Christianity. Later, after

Paul received his call to be an apostle of Jesus Christ, he had to reconcile himself to the fact that he could not change his murderous past so that he could move forward with his new life in Christ (*New King James Version*, 1982, Acts 22:1-21).

At the end of his life, the Apostle Paul provided a summation of his life as he penned the following words: "Brethren, I do not count myself to have apprehended: but one thing I do, forgetting those things which are behind and reaching forward to those things which are ahead, I press toward the goal for the prize of the upward call of God in Jesus Christ" (*New King James Version*, 1982, Philippians 3:13-14). In running my race, to reach the finish line and become the Ventura County Channel League Track and Field champion in the 120-yard high hurdles, I could not remain focused on the past adversities that I experienced or even on the competitors I passed in the process. Following the Apostle Paul's example, I forgot about those things behind, and I reached for those things ahead. What lay ahead of me included the valued league medal, to name just one.

At times, the mean deeds of others can be so horrendous that it seems impossible to forgive or forget. For example, have you ever considered how those falsely accused of a crime felt after spending many years in prison before being pardoned and released after the truth surfaced? Many of these people, rather than remaining angry and bitter, express gratitude when released from jail for the chance to live life outside of prison, which gives them a new lease on life. Also, consider the person who committed horrendous crimes against others who served their complete sentence and were subsequently released from prison. Some of these people now pastor churches, run businesses, and live productive lives. Like those prisoners who were released and found a different life through forgiveness, is it time for you to forgive those who hurt you in the past? Likewise, should you forgive yourself for self-inflicted pain?

Some of you reading this book may have endured painful circumstances, causing you to think about giving up on life. While the pain you faced may have caused you great consternation, I want to encourage you that there is hope as you pray to God to intervene in your situation. The *Holy Bible* records a prayer to God from Jabez (which means Pain; *New King James Version*, 1982, 1 Chron. 4:9-10). The writer of the Book of Chronicles did not share the circumstances behind Jabez's mother calling her son Pain. Some think that she may have experienced complications during his birth or other events in her life before her son's birth that contributed to her giving him such a name.

Whatever the reason(s) involved, Jabez cried out to God for His intervention. Jabez prayed that God would grant him the following:

1. to bless him a lot
2. to expand his territory (or give him a more significant influence in life)
3. to experience the favor of God, and
4. to keep him from experiencing harm or harming others.

Because God found Jabez to be more honorable than his brothers, God answered Jabez's prayer and granted his requests (Wilkinson, 2000). Did you notice that God granted Jabez's requests based on the idea that he was more honorable than his brothers? To say it another way, Jabez was a man that had integrity.

Like Jabez, before I competed in any track and field event, I prayed that God would favor me during the race. The *Holy Bible* admonishes all believers to delight in the Lord, which serves as a precondition for Him to fulfill their heart's desires (*New King James*

Version, 1982, Psalm 37:4). After many years of Bible study, I learned that Psalms 37: 4 does not mean that God is a celestial Santa Claus that gives his children everything they want. However, the prerequisite for a person to receive an answer to their prayer of petition involves seeking God's purposes and living a lifestyle devoted to Him. God will answer the prayer of the believer whose heart aligns with his purposes.

Like the Apostle Paul learned the hard way during his confrontation with Jesus on the road to Damascus when a person learns to stop opposing God, He will take control of their life and change it for His glory. So likewise, the past failures you may have experienced can be turned around and used for God's glory. First, however, may I caution you to remember that the secret to your turnabout involves a life of commitment and service to our Lord and Savior, Jesus Christ.

We all will face our challenges. Some, like the Apostle Paul, will face challenges more severe than most of us will ever have to face, but those challenges are still severe and impact our lives. How we respond to those challenges will make all the difference in whether our lives add up to a W (a win) or an L (a loss). My challenge early in life was how to respond to unexpected interference in a significant track event.

After a competitor spiked me twice as I ran the 120-yard high hurdle race, causing me to fall behind, I overcame those challenges and was now in a comfortable lead. I knew that many underclassmen were watching me, their team captain, regain the lead in the race after coming from behind, and I desired to set a standard for these younger athletes to follow because they would be in the spotlight the following year. At that moment, I wanted to set the bar high for those emerging champions to understand how they should behave in the future.

With my mind clear of all distractions, I continued digging in after leaping over the eighth hurdle. As the Apostle Paul admonished, my focus was not on my past but my future– the prize at the end of the race. My determination to win was more acute than ever before. There was no stopping me now because I was a winner at heart.

The Mindset of an Overcomer

Overcomers conduct regular self-assessment checks to determine they are on target in reaching their desired goals and make the necessary adjustments to remain ahead of their competitors.

Reflective Questions

1. Have you stumbled in your life, allowing a person like Jason (i.e., the senior competitor who practiced with our team) to pass you along the way? Decide to get up, get back in the race, and win.

2. Have you conducted an informal performance management assessment or a performance appraisal? If you have not, do so. You would be surprised at your results.

3. Have you considered your battle of life? Did you overcome it? Or did you stop and give in? Take some time to pray and ask for God's intervention and get back in the game of life.

4. What do you need to do to forget about your past and pursue the prize that lies ahead? First, take some time to pray and ask God to help you renew your perspective in life for his glory and honor.

5. Will you consider doing like Jabez and ask God for his divine intervention regarding the remainder of your life? After doing so, keep a journal of the way(s) that God answers your prayer(s).

Chapter 9

Maintaining Your Competitive Edge

Hurdle #9: Losing Your Competitive Edge
Your competitive edge is what keeps you in the lead. Therefore, never be so generous that you loan, give away, or compromise your ability to remain out front as you compete in life.

In the ninth grade, I ran track and field for the Ventura Boy's Club of America. In the 1970s, the students in Ventura did not begin high school until they reached the ninth grade, unlike many surrounding school districts in neighboring towns and counties. Therefore, what would have been my freshman year of high school and my first year of competitive sports at that level, required that I participate in other organized sports such as playing Pop Warner Football and competing in track and field for the Boy's Club. With inadequate funds to purchase the required equipment needed for their athletes to participate in athletic events and coaches with limited skills, the staff of the Ventura Boys Club took a busload of novice runners to participate in the Boy's Club Invitational Track and Field Meet held in Santa Barbara, CA, at Santa Barbara City College.

One of the events that I competed in was the long jump. I arrived in a pair of tennis shoes on the day of the event. The appropriate footwear worn by track and field athletes was shod with spikes. The small spikes at the bottom of these running shoes allowed a runner or jumper to gain maximum traction in their sporting event. I reached the finals with the second-longest jump. The individual that placed first in the preliminaries was my friend Everett from Santa Maria, California. Everett wore the appropriate spiked shoes to compete in the event. Because we were friends, I asked Everett if I could borrow his track shoes to take my last jump. He consented, so I put his shoes on, tied them up, and risked it all.

While wearing my friend's track shoes, I felt the power from the spikes gripping the tartan runway, which allowed me to reach my maximum speed, which was not attainable when running in a pair of tennis shoes. As I approached the long jump pit, I hit the take-off board like a cheetah's final leap before catching prey. When I heard the announcer say that my jump was over 19 feet, I knew I had won the event and would receive a first-place gold medal. Everett came in second, only to endure the scorn of his teammates as they teased him for allowing another competitor to beat him wearing his shoes. **While I appreciated the generosity of my friend Everett for allowing me to wear his track shoes, I realized that with all things being equal, in doing so, Everett lost his competitive edge–giving me an advantage over him. The lesson I learned from the described transaction was never to give away or lose my competitive edge over a competitor in a situation where I intended to win.**

Finish Strong in Your Race

Fast forward to the 1975 Ventura County Channel League Track and Field Finals race upon which this book is based. As I approached the ninth hurdle, I realized I was approaching the race's climax quickly. I did not want to merely finish the race–but to finish strong. I wanted to finish strong because I wanted to leave a positive legacy behind for posterity's sake. I wanted future generations that did not know me to see that I came from behind to win a race because I was a man of integrity, excellence, and a fighter. **The potential of a positive legacy enables a leader to maintain influence in the eyes of others well into their future. In the business arena, a leader's desire to leave a positive influence for their workers to follow is vital in optimizing the impact of an organization long after the leader that started the enterprise leaves the scene.** Building a positive legacy involves hard work to ensure that the leader leaves their organization more robust, productive, and profitable than when founded. A positive legacy consists of a leader making long-term goals and objectives to benefit the organization over short-term gains (Wade-Benzoni, 2018).

Trainer's Tip #13 – If you want your legacy to provide a positive example that influences others even after your demise, you need to get started now.

My father, the Reverend Luther McCurtis, became friends with a wealthy man in the 1960s named Fritz. Fritz's parents immigrated from Germany during the 1930s. Young Fritz worked for a small tool and dye company on the impoverished side of Ventura, California, which the owner later put up for sale. After saving his money, Fritz earned enough money to purchase the company; Fritz continued to build his small enterprise until he sold it and became the CEO of a much larger offshore drilling company. Over time, he designed and patented a diamond-tipped bit used to drill for oil in an Arctic environment, which led to him becoming a multimillionaire. From that time, Fritz involved himself in many philanthropic endeavors. For example, he donated funds to build a wing for the Ventura Community Memorial Hospital (CMH), where he served as board president for many years. Also, he was instrumental in building a portion of Pepperdine University, located in Malibu, California.

While Fritz was extremely wealthy, he built his home in proximity to his company on the underprivileged side of Ventura. After meeting my dad, Fritz helped fund the construction of the building that housed my father's nonprofit organization, Job Readiness Aptitude and Placement Association (JRAT), later known as the Employment Aptitude and Placement Association (EAPA). Through EAPA, my father provided applicants with free job readiness skills testing and matched those unable to independently secure employment with employment opportunities. Fritz also served as a member of the EAPA's board of directors. Finally, Fritz built a multipurpose room and a fully equipped professional kitchen for my dad's church.

Fritz died in 2018 at the age of 83. His positive legacy succeeds him as a builder of a multibillion-dollar enterprise with a global footprint and a humanitarian who cares for other people's health, education, and quality of life. My father's church and the nonprofit organization continue today, thanks to the generosity of his German friend over the years. How Fritz lived his life as a philanthropist will help future generations receive quality healthcare at CMH and a superior educational experience at Pepperdine University. Moreover, those are only a few examples of Fritz's contributions to society that make up his vast legacy.

Although my father never reached near millionaire status, his work significantly impacted Ventura and Santa Barbara Counties and some nationally and worldwide locations. Dad's work on behalf of the unemployed was so outstanding that in 1982 his exploits as a pastor, humanitarian, and founder of his nonprofit job center came to the attention of the White House. That year, my father was honored to be among only 17 Americans to receive President Ronald Reagan's Volunteer Action Award Medal.

My father passed away on October 8, 2021, at 89 years of age, a few days after I completed this book. He was old and coming to the end of a fruitful and productive life as he transitioned from this earth to Glory. Like the Apostle Paul, who, as he came to the end of his life, penned a letter to Timothy, his young protégé, to encourage him to also live in such a manner that his lifestyle would positively influence others, my father provides the exact words of encouragement to those impacted by his leadership. The passage reads as follows:

> For I am already being poured out as a drink offering, and the time of my departure is at hand. I have fought the good fight, I have finished the race, I have kept the faith. Finally, there is laid up for me the crown of righteousness, which the Lord, the righteous Judge, will give to me on that Day, and not to me only but also to all who have loved His appearing. (*New King James Version*, 1982, 2 Timothy 4:6-8)

From that scripture, I perceived that Paul understood the importance of concluding his life well and providing an example for young Timothy to follow as he began his journey as a new pastor. Paul confidently stated that he had triumphantly reached the end of his life for the following reasons:

1. He was a good soldier of Jesus Christ as he arduously fought against the enemies of God.
2. He remained faithful to the cause of Christ throughout his Christian walk while on earth; he fought a good fight and ran a good race until the end.
3. He was confident he would receive a winner's crown from Jesus Christ.

I ask those of you reading this book, are you satisfied with your life's legacy? Will others say that the example that you set during your life inspires them to follow it? If so, may God richly bless you for the positive example you have displayed. If not, do not lose hope, for all is not lost–you still have time to adjust the trajectory of your life, enabling you, like the Apostle Paul, to fulfill your destiny and to honorably and complete your work here on earth.

Moving Closer to the Finish Line

As I approached the finish line of that race in 1975 that serves as the foundation of this book, I heard those around me yelling their affirmation of my moving closer to victory. Again and again, I could hear, "Go, Gabriel!" Furthermore, I could see the flashing of the cameras' light bulbs from the crowd of people sitting in the stands. Finally, the noise from my coaches, teammates, friends and fans assured me that I was out front and maintaining a comfortable lead.

Now that I am nearing the final stretch of my life here on earth, I decided to return to school and earn a second doctorate. I obtained my first doctorate (i.e., Doctor of Education) from Calvary Chapel University in 2009 at 52. In 2017, at age 60, I launched my effort and matriculated at Southeastern University to earn my second doctorate (i.e., Doctor of Strategic Leadership). While meeting with the cohort of students that comprised the doctoral program, I noticed that I was the second oldest person in the program. One day, an instructor asked the students of our class why we enrolled in the doctoral program. Many answered that a doctorate would enable them to advance further within their employment organizations or to teach at the university level.

In contrast, I informed my fellow students that I was pursuing my doctorate to become a better person and leader. I made this declaration because I was retired and did not need to further my education for upward mobility purposes. Thankfully, I had already achieved many of my goals in life as I culminated in my professional career as a superintendent of schools.

My focus now includes involvement in Total Man International Network, Inc. (TMINI), a nonprofit organization I founded in 2000 to provide community economic development and educational opportunities to families in developing nations. Through the philanthropic arm of TMINI, many young people in Peru receive funding to attend quality schools and universities. In addition, others receive a hot meal daily, and all receive the gospel and learn of the love of Jesus Christ.

The Mindset of an Overcomer

Overcomers strive to build a positive legacy to remain influential on earth after transitioning from this life and entering their eternal abode.

Reflective Questions

1. Can you describe your competitive edge? If so, how do you use it to your advantage? If you are unaware of your competitive edge, take some time to discover it and begin incorporating it into your life.

2. Have you allowed your competitive edge to be used by your competitor? If so, you need to rebrand yourself to incorporate the new you.

3. Upon your demise, will anyone be positively influenced by your legacy? Make a list of these people.

4. Is the legacy that you leave behind optimistic? If your legacy is unfavorable, you should begin developing an improvement plan immediately.

5. Do you know Jesus Christ as your Lord and Savior? If not, would you mind repeating after me the following prayer? "Lord Jesus, forgive me for my sins because I realize I am a sinner. I receive the Blood you shed on Calvary's cross for the atonement of my sins. Come into my heart to dwell forever; I make you my Lord and Savior." If you meant what you just said, you are now born again. Now, I encourage you to find a Bible-believing church so that you can learn more about God and grow into a mature Christian believer.

6. Have you ever read the *Holy Bible*? If not, begin by reading John 3:16 and meditate on what you have read. When finished, read the entire book of John. Now tell a friend that you are now a child of the King. Finally, do not forget to find a Bible-believing church where you can grow spiritually.

Chapter 10

Sprinting Towards the Finish Line

Hurdle #10: Do not Celebrate too Early
The race is not over until you cross the finish line. You may be tempted to celebrate victory prematurely, but do not yield! Otherwise, you may be shocked as a competitor blows by you at the last second! Focus on finishing before you start partying.

As I descended from the tenth hurdle and sprinted toward the finish line, I could see the ribbon, the timers, my coaches, and the press. I could feel the excitement in the air as our cheerleaders met me to cheer me on to victory. As I crossed the finish line and placed first in the race, exhilaration filled my heart. After the other runners crossed the finish line, the head timer informed me that I had run my race in 14.5 seconds, a new school and meet record. What fantastic news! What an accomplishment!

In reflection, my objective was to win the 120-yard high hurdles, give my girlfriend Deborah the medal I won, and move on to the next round of the CIF competition. Unexpectedly, I faced severe adversity to achieve my established goal and objective as another runner interfered twice in my race. Looking down at my right leg, I observed the bleeding spike marks on my knee. Nevertheless, I was so focused on winning that I did not shift my attention from my race to register my discomfort and disdain for the offending hurdler about his behavior in the race. Rather than hurting me and resulting in me losing my race, I now understand that the adversity I endured propelled me to victory and taught me an unforgettable life lesson.

As I have traversed through life, I have found that I compete much harder when facing a disadvantage. That being said, please do not assume I enjoy or welcome adversity. That conclusion would be categorically incorrect. However, when facing severe challenges and challenging circumstances in my professional life and career, I have always found a way to overcome them. For example, three months ago, I lay in a hospital bed after undergoing a five-level spinal fusion to my lumbar area. The amount of pain that I felt after the surgery was excruciating.

Further, I stayed in the hospital for ten days and then transferred to a facility to undergo physical therapy for an additional eight days. My doctor and the attending nurses were surprised by my tenacity while enduring the required physical therapy regimen. They found it unusual to see a senior citizen so motivated to "run to the roar" to reach full recovery. If they asked me to walk up one flight of stairs, I responded by stepping up two additional flights. After being asked to lift a ten-pound weight for three repetitions, I added an extra repetition. After demonstrating that I could meet their requirements, they allowed me to leave the physical therapy facility early because I excelled over the other patients. My intent was never to outshine the other patients; however, I have always set a high bar to attain in life.

How are You Doing Now?

You should always maintain an acute awareness of your performance because such awareness is power. Successful organizations that remain on the cutting edge of business do so because the leadership maintains current knowledge of their organization's performance. For example, all public-school instructors undergo formative and summative evaluations to determine their impact on student learning and achievement in the academic arena. That impact is determined by a battery of educational tests given to students to assess that they have learned and understood the subjects taught. The purpose of a summative assessment determines the amount of learning and academic growth that follows instruction. From the results from the summative instruments used to assess the student population, the measurement of the effectiveness of the educational program(s) supports the decisions that impact future instructional delivery techniques. The summative assessments also identify weak areas and assist in planning to ensure future improvement to attain more favorable results (Baht, 2019).

In the business arena, no organization that reaches its established goals and objectives in the strategic planning process stops and basks in the ambiance after achieving them. **Yes, there is always time to celebrate their successes. Nonetheless, the leadership of these enterprises meets regularly to discuss and evaluate the strategies used in the process, intending to remain at the cutting edge of their business and stay competitive with their rivals. In addition, these leaders find time to assess the entire strategic planning process to determine the strengths and weaknesses of their performance. Finally, during their debriefing sessions, they discuss areas that worked**

and should continue and areas that were problematic and needed to be reviewed with alternative suggestions to try in the future (Miller, 2020).

Setting new goals and objectives for the future is instrumental in keeping you inspired, motivated, and moving forward. With nothing to keep you motivated, you will suffer from a condition known as *entropy* (i.e., a slow dissention into disorder), and you will find your life deteriorating. I own a recreational vehicle (RV) that I keep in storage. When I do not go through the RV periodically to turn on and off appliances, open and close the blinders, and start the engine, I find that some things stop working due to the lack of regular use. You do not want your life to wind down early for the lack of positive use. So, get up and get back into the game of life as you set new health objectives, begin a hobby, and reconnect with your loved ones. Doing so may save your life.

Clearing the Last Hurdle

Each hurdle event involves the runner successfully clearing ten obstacles before crossing the finish line. Whether running the 120-yard high hurdles or the 330-yard low hurdles, each race involves a different running technique; the objective of both races is to successfully clear all barriers. During the 2021 Olympic Games held in Tokyo, Japan, I observed hurdlers favored to win their event lose their races by not successfully clearing the last hurdle. How disappointing the runner must have felt to successfully navigate nine of ten barriers, only to find disaster awaiting them at the final obstacle.

The energy output in any race is significant, but races that involve leaping over hurdles while running long distances place a substantial additional strain on the athlete. For example, the 120-yard high hurdles and the 330-yard low hurdles are exhausting races, but the fatigue factor in the longer distance 330-yard low hurdles presents a much more substantial challenge even though the hurdles are lower in height. That is because the greater the distance in a race, the greater the threat of burnout. Consequently, if the runner burns out before reaching the final hurdle, it will cost them the race. For example, in the 330-yard low hurdle race, as a runner approaches the final hurdle, highly fatigued, the barrier seems ten feet tall. Therefore, a runner must intentionally work to clear the height of the barrier appropriately, or they can fall and fail to complete the race.

Another race that involves jumping over barriers is called the steeplechase. The steeplechase is 3000 meters long with 28 obstacles to overcome and seven jumps across water pits. The height of the obstacles is three feet tall for men and 30 inches in height for women. The water pit immediately following a barrier is two to three feet deep (Magdzik, 2021). While attending UCR, one of my teammates, Mike, ran the steeplechase race. I would watch him clear barrier after barrier and finally land in the water pit. During the first mile of the race, Mike was fresh and cleared each obstacle, seemingly with ease. However, at the end of the race, Mike showed his fatigue as he cleared the last four barriers.

Compared to the steeple chase race, the collegian level high hurdle and intermediate hurdle races are relatively short and considered sprints. In addition, the ten hurdles involved in the collegiate races are lightweight and will not hurt a runner when struck. In contrast, the steeplechase barriers are constructed with solid wood. If a steeplechase runner strikes one of these obstacles, the athlete will sustain a severe injury to their knee. Therefore, a runner competing in any event that involves barriers must approach the final obstacle with optimum and heightened caution to avoid injury and compromise to a successful finish.

Sprinting Towards the Finish Line

The end of every race is the most exciting and, simultaneously, the most fear-provoking. That is because you can see the finish line quickly approaching, but you are keenly aware that your competitors are in hot pursuit of the same prize, inspired by the same sight. After successfully clearing the tenth and final hurdle in my now infamous 1975 Ventura Channel League Track and Field Finals race, I set my mind on finishing the race strong because my high school coaches trained me not to ease up before crossing the finish line. Instead, they taught me to run through the ribbon.

Once again, as I reminisce about the 2021 Olympics, I recall watching runners in the lead raise their hands in celebration before crossing the finish line only to suddenly realize in stunned horror that in a nanosecond, a runner came from behind, overtook and defeated them in the final yards of the race, dashing their dream for Olympic gold and glory. It is natural, understandable, and laudable to celebrate after winning a victory, reaching a goal, or meeting an objective; however, celebrating too early can have devastating consequences and prove very embarrassing when someone presumptuously throws a victory party, then falls short or fails miserably.

What will you do once you accomplish your current goals in life? Will you move on and set new goals and objectives, or will you remain static with no ambitions for the future? Whether you finish well in life is determined by you. Retirement is a significant milestone marking the end of your career, but it does not have to mark the end of your life or your vital contribution in many areas. You have many more years to live with so much more to give. Are you a gardener? Do you like photography, or would you like to learn how to scuba dive?

If you use your mind to learn new things, your mind changes and grows more potent in the same way your muscles increase through exercise (Blackwell, 2014). For those of us who profess Jesus Christ as our Lord and Savior, we do not believe that we have reached the finish line of this life until we hear our Lord and Master say the following words: "Well done, good and faithful servant; you have been faithful over a few things, I will make you ruler over many things. Enter into the joy of your Lord" (*New King James Version*, 1982, Matthew 25:23).

Trainer's Tip #14 – Spending eternity with Jesus and receiving your eternal reward is the only prize worth seeking first.

It is critically important to set goals in their proper order, then work to fulfill them according to their assigned level of importance. That is how I approached the 1975 Ventura County Channel League Track and Field Finals. After crossing the finish line in the 120-yard high hurdles, I completed my first objective of coming in first place. Despite having just won a thrilling victory over seemingly insurmountable odds, and we celebrated accordingly, I did not rest on my laurels. I knew that fulfilling my second objective of winning the 330-yard low hurdles remained temporarily unmet because the race was much later in the track meet. So, I immediately began stretching and preparing for that race. As the time came to compete in the 330-yard low hurdle race, I was mentally and physically prepared to compete at an elite level. I won the race and set a new school and meet record. After meeting both objectives and receiving two first-place awards, I walked away with great satisfaction, having met my main goal of winning two medals to give my girlfriend, Deborah.

Beyond those awesome historical victories, I qualified in three events during the CIF Division Four Prelims, in which I won the 100-yard dash, the 120-yard high hurdles, and the 330-yard low hurdles. Finally in championship fashion, I was blessed to culminate the track season as I competed in the CIF Division Four Finals against some of California's finest track and field runners. So, coming from behind is possible if you maintain the mindset of an overcomer.

The Mindset of an Overcomer

Overcomers do not celebrate their success too early and allow a competitor to overtake them. Instead, they stay focused on pressing forward and winning.

Reflective Questions

1. Do you know your goals and objectives for the remainder of your life? If you do, remain committed to accomplishing them. If not, take some time to write them down and make a plan to achieve them.

3. Do you have a self-evaluation process to determine where you are in life? If so, continue. If not, choose a method of assessment that works for you.

4. Do you have any life hurdles you believe are impossible to clear? If you do, find a support group to assist you in clearing them.

5. Have you begun celebrating before meeting your goals and objectives? I ask you to get back on task and complete each of them.

6. Are you prepared to meet Jesus in peace? Your eternal destiny depends on it. If you have not done so, go back and read reflective question #6 in the previous chapter and pray the sinner's prayer.

Conclusion

As I completed this book, the research enlightened my understanding of the psychology involved when a person that faced adverse circumstances came from behind to regain their lead. The details involved in overcoming life's hurdles were more complicated than I understood as an 18-year-old high school senior. Back then, I did not know the full ramifications of finishing first in the 110-yard high hurdles had on the remainder of my life. At that time, all I knew was that a victory would open the door for me to move to the next level of competition, i.e., the Division Four CIF Prelims held in Santa Barbara, California, and the CIF Finals held at Cerritos High School located in Cerritos, California.

Little did I know, a man sitting in the audience that was the head track and field coach at UCR by the name of Coach Chris was there to observe my performance. His goal was to rebuild his fledgling track team into a powerhouse. Coach Chris noticed that I qualified for CIF in three events:

the 110-yard high hurdles, the 330-yard low hurdles, and the 100-yard dash. As a result of my performance at the CIF Finals, Coach Chris offered me a full athletic scholarship to run for UCR. His offer presented me with a significant opportunity that had profound implications for my life's destiny.

While running at the collegiate level was exciting, my education at one of the finest universities in America was paramount to the academic inculcation that would play a critical role in earning three advanced graduate degrees. Some people who read this book may attribute my journey to this point in life to good luck. At the same time, others may view my success as the culmination of years of hard work. However, I see the struggles I faced while running in the Ventura County Channel League Track and Field Finals as providential.

The interferences I met at the hands of another hurdler, which nearly cost me the race, provided me with a defining moment that led to my destiny in winning the race, attending, and graduating from three different universities, becoming a K-12 administrator, serving as a Church of God in Christ prelate, founding a nonprofit corporation with a global footprint, and now entering a new phase in life as an author, to name a few.

You can also have a similar degree of success if you get back in the game of life and allow God to enable you to be all you can be. In closing, I see you in the future, and your future looks much brighter. Run well, overcome the obstacles that hold you back, get back in the game, and become an overcomer because fulfilling your destiny may positively impact someone else's life.

References

Aazami, A. (2015, June 8). Losing everything is the perfect opportunity [Video]. https://www.youtube.com/watch?v=7qkfKo4m-6A

Adom, A. Y., Nyarko, I. K., & Som, G. N. (2016). Competitor analysis in strategic management: Is it a worthwhile managerial practice in contemporary times? Journal of Resources Development and Management, 24, 116–127. https://core.ac.uk/download/pdf/234696346.pdf

Altuntas, S., & Baykal, U. (2010). Relationship between nurses' organizational trust levels and their organizational citizenship behaviors. Journal of Nursing Scholarship, 42(2), 186–194. https://doi.org/10.1111/j.1547-5069.2010.01347.x

Bagram, M. M., & Altaf, M. (2009). Impact of the transformational leader as change agent on organizational performance and creative solution in a corporation. Interdisciplinary Journal of Contemporary Research in Business, 1(4). https://www.researchgate.net/publication/283054281_Impact_of_Transformational_Leader_as_a_Change_Agent_on_Organizational_Performance_and_Creative_Solution_in_a_Corporate

Baht, B. A. (2019). Formative and summative evaluation techniques for improvement of learning process. European Journal of Business & Social Sciences, 7(5), 776–784. https://www.researchgate.net/publication/333633265_Formative_and_Summative_Evaluation_Techniques_for_Improvement_of_Learning_Process/link/5e6b7e48a6fdccf321d9926e/download

Bandura, A. (1995). Self-efficacy in changing societies. Cambridge University Press. https://doi.org/10.1017/cbo9780511527692

Bass, B. M., & Bass, R. (2008). The Bass handbook of leadership: Theory, research, and managerial applications (4th ed.). Free Press.

Bennett, R. T. (2021). Roy Bennett > quotes > quotables quote. Goodreads. Retrieved July 22, 2021, from https://www.goodreads.com/quotes/7165753-when-you-start-living-the-life-of-your-dreams-there

Bezodis, N., Willwacher, S., & Salo, A. (2019). The biomechanics of the track and field sprint start: A narrative review. Sports Medicine, 49(9), 1345–1364. https://doi.org/10.1007/s40279-019-01138-1

Bies, R. J., Tripp, T. M., Kramer, R. M., & Greenberg, J. (1997). At the breaking point: Cognitive and social dynamics of revenge in organizations. In R. Giacalone (Ed.), Antisocial behavior in organizations (pp. 18–36). Sage.

Blackwell, L. (2014). New research shows the brain can be developed like a muscle. Prepare for success. Retrieved October 1, 2021, from https://www.cmich.edu/ess/oss/documents/prepare%20for%20success%20d4.pdf

Blau, P. M. (1964). Exchange and power in social life. Wiley.

Brewer, B. W. (2009). Sport psychology. John Wiley & Sons. https://doi.org/10.1002/9781444303650
Broadhurst, P. L. (1957). Emotionality and the Yerkes-Dodson law. Journal of Experimental Psychology, 54(5), 345–352. https://doi.org/10.1037/h0049114

Bull, S. J., Albinsom, J. G., & Shambrook, C. J. (1996). The mental game plan: Getting psyched for sport. Sport Dynamics.

Burns, J. (1978). Leadership (1st ed.). Harper and Row Publishers. (Original work published 1978)

Cheng, J. T., Tracy, J. L., & Henrich, J. (2010). Pride, personality, and the evolutionary foundations of human social status. Evolution and Human Behavior, 31(5), 334–347. https://doi.org/10.1016/j.evolhumbehav.2010.02.004

Chirkov, V., Ryan, R. M., Kim, Y., & Kaplan, U. (2003). Differentiating autonomy from individualism and independence: A self-determination theory perspective on internalization of cultural orientations and well-being. Journal of Personality and Social Psychology, 84(1), 97–110. https://doi.org/10.1037/0022-3514.84.1.97

Cho, J. (2006). The mechanism of trust and distrust formation and their relational outcomes. Journal of Retailing, 82(1), 25–35. https://doi.org/10.1016/j.jretai.2005.11.002

Cropanzano, R., Anthony, E. L., Daniels, S. R., & Hall, A. V. (2017). Social exchange theory: A critical review with theoretical remedies. Academy of Management Annals, 11(1), 479–516. https://doi.org/10.5465/annals.2015.0099

Cummings, L. L., & Bromiley, P. (2012). The organizational trust inventory (OTI): Development and validation. In Trust in organizations: Frontiers of theory and research (pp. 302–330). SAGE Publications. https://doi.org/10.4135/9781452243610.n15

Davis, J. H. (1996). Managing and achieving organizational goals. American Management Association.

Downton, J. V. (1973). Rebel leadership: Commitment and charisma in the revolutionary process. Free Press.

Eisenberger, R., Fasolo, P., & Davis-LaMastro, V. (1990). Perceived organizational support and employee diligence, commitment, and innovation. Journal of Applied Psychology, 75(1), 51–59. https://doi.org/10.1037/0021-9010.75.1.51

Ericsson, K., Krampe, R. T., & Tesch-Römer, C. (1993). The role of deliberate practice in the acquisition of expert performance. Psychological Review, 100(3), 363–406. https://doi.org/10.1037/0033-295x.100.3.363

Ericsson, K., Nandagopal, K., & Roring, R. W. (2009). Toward a science of exceptional achievement. Annals of the New York Academy of Sciences, 1172(1), 199–217. https://doi.org/10.1196/annals.1393.001

Fletcher, D., & Sarkar, M. (2012). A grounded theory of psychological resilience in Olympic champions. Psychology of Sport and Exercise, 13(5), 669–678. https://doi.org/10.1016/j.psychsport.2012.04.007

Fonteneau, Y., Hughes, L., Rampersad, A., & Roessel, D. (1996). The collected poems of Langston Hughes. World Literature Today, 70(1), 192. https://doi.org/10.2307/40151942

Franklin, B., Wooden, J., Schuller, R. H., Williams, H. K., HOPE, J. H., & Gregory, E. B. (2018, July 8). If you fail to prepare, you are preparing to fail. Quoterresearch. Retrieved September 7, 2021, from https://quoteinvestigator.com/2018/07/08/plan/

Fulmer, C., & Gelfand, M. (2012). At what level (and in whom) we trust: Trust across multiple organizational levels. Journal of Management, 38(4), 1167–1230. https://doi.org/10.2139/ssrn.1873149

Gillen, T. (2007). Performance management and appraisal. Kogan Page.

Givens, R. J. (2008). Transformational leadership: The impact on organizational and personal outcomes. Emerging Leadership Journeys, 1(1), 4–24. https://www.regent.edu/acad/global/publications/elj/issue1/ELJ_V1Is1_Givens.pdf

goDeskless. (2020, October 28). Don't be the next Blockbuster: Learning from companies who failed to innovate. Retrieved September 15, 2021, from https://godeskless.com/blog/learning-from-companies-who-failed-to-innovate/

Gospel Nostalgia. (2012, August 5). 99 and a Half, Just Won't Do [Video]. YouTube. https://www.youtube.com/watch?v=NIytd0J91RU

Gould, D., Dieffenbach, K., & Moffett, A. (2002). Psychological characteristics and their development in Olympic champions. Journal of Applied Sport Psychology, 14(3), 172–204. https://doi.org/10.1080/10413200290103482
Gould, D., Hodge, K., Peterson, K., & Petlichkoff, L. (1987). Psychological foundations of coaching: Similarities and differences among intercollegiate wrestling coaches.

The Sport Psychologist, 1(4), 293–308.
https://doi.org/10.1123/tsp.1.4.293

Groom, W. (1986). Forrest Gump. Doubleday.

Guest, E. A. (2007). Collected works of Edgar A. Guest. BiblioBazaar. https://www.best-poems.net/edgar_albert_guest/see_it_through.html

Hebb, D. O. (1955). Drives and the c. n. s. (conceptual nervous system). Psychological Review, 62(4), 243–254. https://doi.org/10.1037/h0041823

Hermalin, B. E. (1997). Toward an economic theory of leadership: Leading by example. SSRN Electronic Journal. https://doi.org/10.2139/ssrn.15570

Hickman, D. C., & Metz, N. E. (2015). The impact of pressure on performance: Evidence from the PGA tour. Journal of Economic Behavior & Organization, 116, 319–330. https://doi.org/10.1016/j.jebo.2015.04.007

Howells, K., Sarkar, M., & Fletcher, D. (2017). Can athletes benefit from difficulty? A systematic review of growth following adversity in competitive sport. In Progress in brain research (pp. 117–159). Elsevier. https://doi.org/10.1016/bs.pbr.2017.06.002

Hughes, D. C., Ellefsen, S., & Baar, K. (2017). Adaptations to endurance and strength training. Cold Spring Harbor Perspectives in Medicine, 8(6), a029769.
https://doi.org/10.1101/cshperspect.a029769

Ikulayo, P. B. (1990). Understanding sports psychology. Eaiton Press.

Insko, C. A., & Schopler, J. (1997). Differential distrust of groups and individuals. In C. Sedikides, J. Schopler, & C. Insko (Eds.), Intergroup cognition and intergroup behavior (pp. 75–108). Erlbaum.

Karimi, S. (2017, March 8). How to mentally recover after a financial setback: A major money mistake doesn't have to take a toll on your well-being. US News. Retrieved September 4, 2021, from https://money.us-news.com/money/blogs/my-money/articles/2017-03-08/how-to-mentally-recover-after-a-financial-setback

Krot, K., & Lewicka, D. (2012). The importance of trust in manager-employee relationships. The International Journal of Electronic Business Management, 10(3), 224–233. https://www.researchgate.net/publication/319130798_THE_IMPORTANCE_OF_TRUST_IN_MANAGER-EMPLOYEE_RELATIONSHIPS

Lauer, L., & Blue, K. (n.d.). The 3 c's of being a captain. Association for Applied Sport Psychology. Retrieved August 31, 2021, from https://appliedsportpsych.org/resources/resources-for-athletes/the-3-c-s-of-being-a-captain/

Lei, D., & Slocum, J. W. (2005). Strategic and organizational requirements for competitive advantage. Academy of Management Perspectives, 19(1), 31–45. https://doi.org/10.5465/ame.2005.15841949

Levi, M., Moe, M., & Buckley, T. (2004). The transaction costs of distrust: Labor and management at the National Labor Relations Board. In R. Hardin (Ed.), Distrust (pp. 106–135). Russel Sage Foundation.

Liew, G., Kuan, G., Chin, N., & Hashim, H. (2019). Mental toughness in sport. German Journal of Exercise and Sport Research, 49(4), 381–394. https://doi.org/10.1007/s12662-019-00603-3

Magdziuk, K. (2021, July 29). What is the steeplechase event at the Olympics? Draft Kings Nation. Retrieved October 1, 2021, from https://dknation.draftkings.com/olympics/2021/7/29/22600803/what-is-steeplechase-tokyo-summer-oylmpics-2021-track-and-field-athletics-race

Magyar-Moe, J. L., & Lopez, S. J. (2015). Strategies for accentuating hope. In S. Joseph (Ed.), Positive psychology in practice: Promoting human flourshing in work, health, education, and everyday life (2nd ed., pp. 483–502). Wiley.

Maslow, A. H. (1954). Motivation and personality. Harper and Row.

Masten, A. S. (2001). Ordinary magic: Resilience processes in development. American Psychologist, 56(3), 227–238. https://doi.org/10.1037/0003-066x.56.3.227

Maxwell, J. C. (2002). Teamwork makes the dream work. Thomas Nelson.

Miller, K. (2020, February 26). A manager's guide to successful strategy implementation. Harvard Business School Online. Retrieved October 1, 2021, from https://online.hbs.edu/blog/post/strategy-implementation-for-managers

Morris, A. (2021). Developing confidence in sports. BelievePerform Mental Health & Wellbeing. Retrieved June 23, 2021, from https://believeperform.com/developing-confidence-in-sport/

Northouse, P. G. (2019). Leadership: Theory and practice (8th ed.). Sage.

Ohuruogu, B., Abakaliki, U. I., & Ikechukwu, U. J. (2016). Psychological preparation for peak performance in sports competition. Journal of Education and Practice, 7(12), 47–50. https://files.eric.ed.gov/fulltext/EJ1099480.pdf

Prajapati, R., Sharma, B., & Sharma, D. (2016). Significance of life skills education. Contemporary Issues in Education Research (CIER), 10(1), 1–6. https://doi.org/10.19030/cier.v10i1.9875

Pučėtaitė, R., Lämsä, A., & Novelskaitė, A. (2010). Building organizational trust in a low-trust societal context. Baltic Journal of Management, 5(2), 197–217. https://doi.org/10.1108/17465261011045124

Saul, L. J., & Rickman, J. (1940). A general selection from the works of Sigmund Freud. The Psychoanalytic Quarterly, 9(3), 415–443. https://doi.org/10.1080/21674086.1940.11925435

Saunders, M., & Thornhill, A. (2004). Trust and mistrust in organizations: An exploration using an organizational justice framework. European Journal of Work and Organizational Psychology, 13(4), 493–515. https://doi.org/10.1080/13594320444000182

Serrano, J., Shahidian, S., Sampaio, J., & Leite, N. (2013). The importance of sports performance factors and training contents from the perspective of futsal coaches. Journal of Human Kinetics, 38, 151–160. https://doi.org/10.2478/hukin-2013-0055

SHRM. (2010). Performance management and appraisal. SHRM HR Content. Retrieved September 14, 2021, from https://www.sagepub.com/sites/default/files/upm-binaries/45674_8.pdf

Singh, R. (2016). The impact of intrinsic and extrinsic motivators on employee engagement in information organizations. Journal of Education for Library and Information Science Online, 57(2), 197–206. https://doi.org/10.12783/issn.2328-2967/57/2/11

Skinner, B. R. (2013). The relationship between confidence and performance throughout a competitive season (285) [Master's thesis, Utah State University]. All Graduate Plan B and other Reports. https://digitalcommons.usu.edu/gradreports/285

Slimelane, Z. P., & Mafumbate, R. (2019). Life skills education for enhancement of learners' wellness in Eswatini: A case of high school learners in Shiselweni region. Journal of Resources Development and Management, 44–50. https://doi.org/10.7176/jrdm/59-06

Smith, C. (2017, October 2). Luke 18:1-8 - In-depth [Speech audio recording]. CalvaryTruths.com. https://youtu.be/o3g3LhufNVE

Snyder, L. L., & Morris, R. M. (2021). "I have not yet begun to fight," 1779: John Paul Jones in Battle. EyeWitness to History.com. Retrieved August 23, 2021, from http://www.eyewitnesstohistory.com/johnpauljones.htm

Soul Salt. (2021, March 22). How to be your authentic self: 7 powerful strategies to be true. How to be your authentic self: Powerful strategies to be true. Retrieved August 10,

2021, from https://soulsalt.com/how-to-be-your-authentic-self/

Sull, D. (1999). Organizational culture: Why good companies go bad. Harvard Business Review. Retrieved September 11, 2021, from https://doi.org/https://hbr.org/1999/07/why-good-companies-go-bad

The psychology of commitment, absenteeism, and turnover. (1982). In Mowday, R. T., Porter, L. W., & Steers, R. M. (Eds.), Employee–organization linkages (pp. 245–250). Academic Press. https://doi.org/10.1016/b978-0-12-509370-5.50015-0

Tracy, J. L., & Robins, R. W. (2007). Emerging insights into the nature and function of pride. Current Directions in Psychological Science, 16(3), 147–150. https://doi.org/10.1111/j.1467-8721.2007.00493.x

Ullmann-Margalit, E. (2004). Trust, distrust, and in-between. In R. Harding (Ed.), Distrust (pp. 60–82). Russel Sage Foundation.

Vanhala, M., Heilmann, P., & Salminen, H. (2016). Organizational trust dimensions as antecedents of organizational commitment. Knowledge and Process Management, 23(1), 46–61. https://doi.org/10.1002/kpm.1497
Weinberg, R. S., & Gould, D. (2003). foundations of sport and exercise psychology. Champaign: Human Kinetics.

Wikipedia. (2021, August 16). The rumble in the jungle. Wikipedia: The Free Encyclopedia. Retrieved September 13, 2021, from https://en.wikipedia.org/wiki/The_Rumble_in_the_Jungle

Wilkinson, B. (2000). The prayer of Jabez. Multnomah Publishers.

Williams, C. (2012). MGMT (5th ed.). Southwest College Publishing.

Winston, B. E., & Patterson, K. (2006). An integrative definition of leadership. International Journal of Leadership Studies, 1(2), 6–66. https://www.regent.edu/acad/global/publications/ijls/new/vol1iss2/winston_patterson.doc/winston_patterson.pdf

Yeager, D., & Dweck, C. S. (2012). Mindsets that promote resilience: When students believe that personal characteristics can be developed. Educational Psychologist, 47(4), 302–314. https://doi.org/10.1080/00461520.2012.722805

Zahra, S. A., & Chaples, S. S. (1993). Blind spots in competitive analysis. Academy of Management Perspectives, 7(2), 7–28. https://doi.org/10.5465/ame.1993.9411302318

Appendix A - Lessons Learned from Life's Hurdles

- **Hurdle #1: Inadequate Preparation** - Avoid entering your competition unprepared to compete at your best mentally, physically, and emotionally.

- **Hurdle #2: Being Unprepared to Handle Contingencies** - Expect the unexpected and prepare yourself to overcome all unforeseen problems.

- **Hurdle #3: Resisting Arrogant Pride** - Arrogance and conceit will try to captivate your soul but resist the temptation at all costs.

- **Hurdle #4: The Loss of Faith & Hope** - Losing your faith and hope results in discouragement that will compel you to give up and quit, but do not give in to its influence.

- ❖ **Hurdle #5: The Testing of Your Leadership Ability** - Without a doubt, your leadership ability will be tested. To clear the hurdle necessary to become an inspirational and impactful leader, you must develop your leadership acumen and purpose to help those you lead become their best selves.

- ❖ **Hurdle #6: Your Lead Will be Challenged** - Failing to remain focused after losing your lead in a competition can compromise your ability to regain the lead.

- ❖ **Hurdle #7: Reliance Upon Past Successes to Resolve New Challenges** - Resist the temptation to rest on past success(es) because your past success(es) is only helpful if you use the information you gained in it to face the new set of challenges you will undoubtedly face in all your future races.

- ❖ **Hurdle #8: Overcoming the Battle of Life -** You will face your battle of life. Win it, and the world will swing wide its doors to you. Lose it, and the world will shut you out of a lifetime of opportunities that were designed for you. Therefore, fight to win at all costs; your future depends on it.

❖ **Hurdle #9: Losing Your Competitive Edge** - Your competitive edge is what keeps you in the lead. Therefore, never be so generous that you loan, give away, or compromise your ability to remain out front as you compete in life.

❖ **Hurdle #10: Do not Celebrate too Early** - The race is not over until you cross the finish line. You may be tempted to celebrate victory prematurely, but do not yield! Otherwise, you may be shocked as a competitor blows by you at the last second! Focus on finishing before you start partying.

Appendix B - Trainer's Tips

- #1 - There are times when you will not reach your expectations. Do not be alarmed, as this is a part of life.

- #2 - As you journey through life, be prepared to experience unforeseen interferences and occurrences.

- # 3 - To overcome adversity, you must maintain a positive outlook and remain in the game.

- #4 - Your preparedness to adequately face and respond to life's adversities will have an impact on how you deal with them.

- #5 - Perseverance is a crucial factor in overcoming adversity.

- #6 - You should always be proud that you did something well (i.e., achievement). However, personal pride should never lead to arrogance or conceit.

- #7 - Being authentic requires that your public persona is appropriately aligned to your private self.
- #8 - Your self-talk influences your accomplishments; therefore, keep your self-talk positive.
- #9 - Your leadership acumen can open or close the doors to key opportunities.
- #10 - Never allow someone to take the lead you once had without putting up a fierce fight to regain it.
- #11 - To remain competitive, you must become a lifelong learner–one who is open to personal improvement and one who embraces change.
- #12 - Everyone must confront and overcome their battle of life.
- #13 - If you want your legacy to provide a positive example that influences others even after your demise, you need to get started now.

- **#14 - Spending eternity with Jesus and receiving your eternal reward is the most important prize worth seeking first.**

Appendix C - The Mindset of an Overcomer

1) Overcomers prevail and conquer their obstacles and hurdles despite setbacks by maintaining a never-give-up and never-give-in mentality.

2) Overcomers understand that there are opportunities on the other side of adversity that are not attainable if they quit prematurely and give up in the pursuit.

3) Overcomers are not pridefully self-reliant. They understand that along with their hard work, placing their trust in God for the thing(s) they hope will come to pass is of the utmost importance.

4) Overcomers maintain an "I still can win" attitude after facing adversity that caused them to fall behind the pack.

5) Overcomers understand that leaders are in a position of trust; therefore, leadership is a calling that should be handled with diligence, finesse, and dedication.

6) Overcomers understand that there is still life after they have suffered loss, so they strive to make the best of a bad situation.

7) Overcomers understand that it takes hard work to accomplish anything in life, especially to recover from a loss. Therefore, there is never time for complacency.

8) Overcomers conduct regular self-assessment checks to determine they are on target in reaching their desired goals and make the necessary adjustments to remain ahead of their competitors.

9) Overcomers strive to build a positive legacy to remain influential on earth after transitioning from this life and entering their eternal abode.

10) Overcomers do not celebrate their success too early and allow a competitor to overtake them. Instead, they stay focused on pressing forward and winning.

Coaching Experience

Thank you for reading my book! If you need help to overcome **unexpected career challenges to get back on track, achieve your next career goal, and equip yourself to reach your maximum potential**, I can help you in your endeavor. As a professional transformational coach, an outline of my flagship transformational coaching experience program is listed below:

"Your Destiny Reimagined: A 90-Day Transformational Coaching Experience for Professionals to Overcome Career Challenges."

I. Coping with the past and reimagining a new future
1. Unpacking your career path
2. Making peace with the challenges that interrupted your goals
3. Developing the Pride of Achievement, not Arrogance

II. Setting Your Future Through Powerful Thinking

1. Reframing Your Responses for Maximal Results
2. Moving From Perfection to Excellence
3. Attaining the Mindset of an Overcomer

III. Becoming a Force to Be Reckoned With
1. Developing Determination Through Bull Dog Tenacity
2. Leading Effectively by Helping Others to Reach Their Dream
3. Stepping Into Your Desired Destiny and Sprinting Towards the Finish Line

For more information about the 90-day transformational coaching experience program, you may contact Dr. McCurtis at gmccurtis@gmail.com to schedule a free strategy session.

About the Author

Gabriel E. McCurtis, Ed.D., DSL, is a retired K-12 superintendent of schools. McCurtis completed his BA and MA degrees at the University of California, Riverside (1975-1983), a Doctor of Education (Ed.D.) from Calvary Chapel University (2009-2012), and a Doctor of Strategic Leadership (DSL) from Southeastern University (2018-2021), where he was inducted into the Florida Lambda Chapter of Alpha Chi, a National College Honor Scholarship Society. McCurtis has been married to Mrs. Deborah McCurtis since 1977. He has three adult daughters: O. Renee Barron (husband Douglas Barron, Sr.), Olympia McCurtis, Jennifer McCurtis, seven grandchildren, and a great-grandchild on the way.

About the Publisher

The VTF Group offers a variety of publishing options.

The VTF Group has earned its positive reputation because we go out of our way to provide truly exceptional service to each of our customers, something we like to call - "The White Glove Experience."

We believe that publishing a book is about more than becoming an author. It is about bringing a vision to fruition, building an audience, and expanding your influence.

Not all publishers are created equal, and we know that when extra attention is required, our "White Glove Experience" will not disappoint.

As an experienced team of authors, we also specialize in coaching you through the publishing process and bringing your vision to fruition.

Contact us today to schedule a free 15-minute consultation via: www.TheVTFGroup.com

Made in the USA
Las Vegas, NV
09 January 2023